KT-481-002

THEORIES
OF THE MIXED ECONOMY

THEORIES
OF
THE MIXED ECONOMY

Edited by
DAVID REISMAN

VOLUME III

A. C. PIGOU

Socialism versus Capitalism

LONDON
WILLIAM PICKERING
1994

Published by Pickering & Chatto (Publishers) Limited
17 Pall Mall, London, SW1Y 5NB

© Pickering & Chatto (Publishers) Limited
Introduction © David Reisman

All rights reserved. No part of this publication may be
reproduced, stored in a retrieval system, or transmitted in
any form or by any means, electronic, mechanical,
photocopying, recording, or otherwise without prior permission
of the publisher.

British Library Cataloguing in Publication Data
Theories of the Mixed Economy. – Vol. III:
Socialism Versus Capitalism. – New ed
  I. Reisman, David II. Pigou, Arthur
  330.126
Set ISBN 1 85196 213 1
This volume ISBN 1 85196 216 6

Printed and bound in Great Britain by
Antony Rowe Limited
Chippenham

CONTENTS

A C PIGOU

Arthur Cecil Pigou was born on 18 November 1877 at Ryde, Isle of Wight. His father was a retired army officer.

Like his father, Pigou was educated at Harrow School, attending on an entrance scholarship. He excelled in athletics as well as academic subjects and was Head Boy. He then read history at Kings College, Cambridge, where he was awarded his BA with First Class Honours in 1899. He won the Chancellor's medal for English verse in the same year. In 1900 (while serving at the same time as President of the Union) he was awarded a further First, in Part II of the Moral Sciences Tripos. Ethics was a part of the Tripos. So was economics. The textbook was Marshall's *Principles*, published in 1890 and already in its fourth revision. The Professor was Marshall himself, increasingly aware in his late fifties that without disciples his crusade might not be for all seasons.

In 1901 Pigou began to lecture on economics – more as a generalist than a specialist and with a background in history and philosophy rather than the mathematical abstractions with which he was never really to be entirely comfortable. In 1902 he was made a Fellow at King's. He was in the right place at the right time: in 1903 Marshall finally succeeded in pushing through the new, specialist Economics Tripos, and Pigou (who had supported the Professor on the primacy of professionalisation) was appointed to the Girdlers' Lectureship, from 1904. Also in 1903 came the bitter controversy about the reimposition of tariffs that in effect pitted the neoclassical economists against the nationalists of the Historical School on the question of the freedom of trade. Pigou, like Marshall, campaigned actively against the new protectionism despite the acknowledged encroachment of 'Made in Germany'. His first book, *The Riddle of the Tariff* (1903), was his intellectual contribution to the debate.

In 1908, aged only 30, Pigou was elected to the Chair of Political Economy at Cambridge. The two other contenders for Marshall's professorship, Ashley and Foxwell, 48 and 58 respectively, were better known than the candidate of promise and potential whose major publications had been a short paper on utility in the *Economic Journal* for 1903, the polemic on the *Riddle*, and the speculative and unsupported *Principles and Methods of Industrial Peace* of 1905. Ashley and Foxwell were empiricists and protectionists, sceptical about pure theory and opposed to free trade. Pigou was an uncritical expositor of the master's analytics, an enthusiastic follower whose standard response to generations of undergraduates (he taught the second-year core course in advanced economic theory for more than three decades) was that 'it's all in Marshall'. Without in any way detracting from the importance of what Pigou himself was later to accomplish in the 37 years that separated his appointment to the Chair from his retirement in 1943 (to say nothing of the further 16 years that separated his retirement from his death on 7 March 1959), it is impossible to escape the conclusion that it was at least in part for Marshall Part II that electors such as Edgeworth and J N Keynes were voting when in 1908 they opted for continuity even as they opted for excellence.

As with Marshall, Pigou was a man of 'social enthusiasm', committed to a useful economics of 'fruit' in preference to a self-indulgent pyrotechnics that produced only 'light'. His strong moral principles extended to the world outside the Quad: in the First World War, unprepared to take a human life, he did not volunteer for military service although still of military age. He did, on the other hand, put himself forward for ambulance service at the Front (quite a dangerous way to spend the Cambridge vacations between his teaching terms). In 1918–19 Pigou was a member of the Cunliffe Committee on currency and foreign exchange; in 1919–20 of the Royal Commission on the Income Tax; in 1924–5 of the Chamberlain Committee on the Bank of England and the note-issue. He was a supporter in the early 1920s of an early return to gold and – irrespective of the disruption to growth and employment that this might cause – of the restoration of the pre-1914 exchange-rate. Pigou's insensitivity to quantity-adjustments (as opposed to wage-flexibilities and price changes) was to bring him into conflict with another King's Fellow, his former student, J M Keynes. It was not the last time that this would happen. Keynes's *General Theory* in 1936 announced that Pigou's *Theory of Unemployment* of 1933 had managed to 'get out of the Classical Theory all that can be got out of it' – and that still it offered no practicable solution to the social tragedy of under-employment equilibrium. Pigou replied at length in his 17-page *Economica* review of Keynes's book; in his *Employment and Equilibrium* (1941); and in the two later papers – 'The Classical Stationary State' (*Economic Journal*, 1943) and 'Economic Progress in a Stable Environment' (*Economica*, 1947) – in which (acknowledging the impracticality of across-the-board deflation and recognising the possibility of perverse expectations engendering speculative hoarding) he argued that falling money prices, rising real balances, would in themselves provide for a self-correcting mechanism in the form of a diminished need to abstain from consumption. Later Pigou was to become more sympathetic to the income-expenditure approach. The lectures delivered in the year of Keynes's death and published as *Keynes' 'General Theory': A Retrospective View* (1950) show just how much of demand-expansion in place of wage-cuts he was ultimately able to accept.

Pigou, interestingly, had been in favour of public spending long before Keynes had begun to write on stabilisation and jobs. In his Inaugural Address of 1908, in his *Unemployment* (1913), Pigou had rejected the 'Treasury View' of theorists of futility such as R G Hawtrey in *Good and Bad Trade* (1913), that public works could not expand output and employment as they would simply divert to the State sector resources that would otherwise have been spent by private parties. Pigou did not recommend a budget deficit, neither in his early writings nor when he returned to expansionary policies in his *Industrial Fluctuations* (1927), *A Study in Public Finance* (1928) and *The Economics of Stationary States* (1935). What he did suggest is that even a balanced budget could be stimulatory precisely because the taxes that finance the interventions fall at least in part on 'funds which would normally have been stored'. Besides that, and even if the taxes do no more than transfer the spending, at least the sum of social satisfaction must rise when resources are channelled to the relatively deprived that 'would normally have been consumed by the relatively well-to-do'. A champion of social justice as well as an advocate of full employment, Pigou on public works appears to be endorsing policies that were later to be associated as much with the Fabian socialists as with the macroeconomic fiscalists.

Pigou, like Marshall, was anxious to do good – and to do good, quite specifically, through the medium of political economy. His concern with upgrading and redistribution, in evidence in his books and papers on stabilisation and jobs, comes most clearly into its own in his *Wealth and Welfare* (1912) and in the four editions (of 1920, 1924, 1929, 1932) of its successor, *The Economics of Welfare*, far and away Pigou's most influential work. In it, and adopting Marshall's procedure of approximating subjective satisfaction with the measuring rod of money, Pigou (while not neglecting the neoclassical themes of allocative efficiency and price-determination) returned to Smith on the wealth of nations by insisting that a growth in economic welfare may reasonably be taken as a rise in total welfare too. The national dividend is a welfare indicator, Pigou maintained; but so (as a consequence of the established Marshallian imputation of diminishing utility to additional income) must be the distribution of that product as between the absolutely comfortable and the absolutely needy. Pigou sought to combine his aggregative macro-dynamics (a source of inspiration to the Keynesians and the growth-men) with his commitment to the greater equality of income and wealth (a warning to the socialists that even liberal utilitarians could be dissatisfied with the *laissez-faire* verdict on social distance). From the premium on expansion in alliance with the endorsement of levelling then followed the inevitable conclusion: 'Any cause which increases the absolute share of real income in the hands of the poor, provided that it does not lead to a contraction in the national dividend from any point of view, will, in general, increase economic welfare'. Pigou's maximising deductivism legitimated the social services State of education and health, progressive income tax and perhaps also a minimum wage law. It presupposed, of course, that people were sufficiently alike on average for inter-personal comparisons to serve as the meaningful basis for practical policy. If they are not, then Pigou's positive analysis of social justice must give way to a more normative – and a more controversial – defence of the State as an economic Robin Hood.

Searching as he was for the point of maximum felicity, Pigou in *The Economics of Welfare* made an important distinction between the marginal private net product (the individual return that the free play of informed self-interest tends in competitive equilibrium harmoniously to equalise) and the marginal social net product (the collective benefit or loss that is the private product plus or minus the externalities and the spillovers that are not picked up by the originator's calculus). Private investment will be excessive where the entrepreneur's product is greater than the neighbourhood's gain (the case of a smoking chimney that imposes the uncompensated diswelfare of additional laundry). Private commitment will be deficient where the incremental attraction to the part is less than the incremental utility of the whole (the case where the nation wants high-productivity farming but the tenant on a short lease has a sub-optimal incentive to improve). Private expenditure will, however, be welfare-maximising where the marginal private net product is equal to the marginal social net product (and, by extension, the marginal social net product is equal in all uses of a given resource): there and there alone will the calculus be complete as there and there alone will the unit that receives all the gains also be the decision-maker that bears all the costs. Admirable in itself, the invisible hand was incapable, un-assisted, of producing the maximising result. The market was indispensable. So too, however, was the enlightened guidance of the taxing, subsidising, regulating State that, Marshall-like, put right a market failure.

Sympathetic to the State, Pigou was a non-socialist who read the Fabians with interest and shared much of the vision that had caused Tawney, Dalton and the Webbs to associate the inevitability of gradualness with the inevitability of politicisation. *Socialism versus Capitalism* (1937) was his attempt to clarify in his own mind just where his middle way actually led him in respect of the alternative economic orders. It led him, not surprisingly, to the open verdict of the natural pragmatist.

On the social side, Pigou was in agreement with the socialists that contemporaneous disparities in income and wealth were 'a grave social evil' that had to be corrected through the equalisation both of opportunities (including State-provided health and education such as break the vicious circle of inter-generational poverty) and of endstates (including graduated death-duties, steep income tax and public subsidisation of commodities consumed disproportionately by the poor). Economics was more tricky; but bounties and duties to equalise private and social benefits were clearly an eminently Pigovian fulcrum for authority. Perhaps revealing his irreducible libertarian-ism, Pigou when faced with the challenge of implementation rapidly retreated into the cautious evasiveness of a man unsure: 'The diffi-culties are formidable', he admitted, the State lacks the data, and not even the best planners can put a precise value on real-world spill-overs such as the indirect benefits to the climate that result from the planting of a forest. Theory may validate intervention, Pigou seems to have been saying, but internalising policy must nonetheless be dependent on a degree of knowledge that the policy-maker may simply not possess.

Central direction is at any rate on solid ground when it seeks to challenge the market dominance of the natural monopoly. Pigou looked to the State for the supervision and regulation of scale-intensive industries (rail-transport, water-supply, gas, electricity) where competition could not be relied upon for moderate profits and dynamic efficiency. He also went as far as to call for public owner-ship and operation in areas such as the commanding heights of the Bank of England and the manufacture of armaments. Assuming satisfactory performance, he was convinced, other 'important indus-tries' would follow later, gradually, cautiously and 'by degrees'. Marshall had generally been sceptical about nationalisation on the grounds that it would be a threat to invention, novelty and initiative, *prima facie* anti-social and a brake on growing wealth. Pigou's posi-tion was less cautious. On the one hand there was the capitalist corporation, the creature of business bureaucrats afraid to take risks, the cause of intolerable waste through competitive advertising. On the other hand there was the public corporation, adventurous be-cause the State favours change, independent because outside com-missioners appreciate the need for operational autonomy. Marshall, Pigou said, had made the mistake of assuming that all State-owned assets had to be administered (like the Post Office) directly by a ministry. The new-style public corporation would have caused him to re-think his attitude to socialism versus capitalism and to the public interest in the era of imperfect competition.

Business and State had moved on since Marshall. So had the political economy of unemployment. Wage-cuts and not aggregate demand policies remained the *sine qua non* for returning the nation to work: to that extent the Pigou of 1937 was every inch the 'classical economist' that he had been in 1933. Yet Pigou was a non-Keynesian who was undeniably favourable to the intervention of a leaderly State. Planners have the edge over markets in coordinating the reductions in pay. Indicative forecasts restrict industrial fluctuations that unmatched supplies might otherwise have exacerbated. Pecuni-ary relief prevents the social cost of dismissal from falling on the worker alone. Public works create a limited number of jobs at a time when private investment is insensitive even to a rock-bottom rate of interest. Pigou does not say that all this adds up to an endorsement of central direction in preference to the price mechanism. What he does suggest is that there is a role for both the market and the State in the pragmatically-mixed compromise. In that sense a better title for *Socialism versus Capitalism* would probably be *Socialism Together with Capitalism – The Middle Way*.

FURTHER READING

Primary

'A Parallel between Economic and Political Theory', *Economic Journal*, Vol 12, 1902

'The Unity of Political and Economic Science', *Economic Journal*, Vol 16, 1906

Wealth and Welfare (London: Macmillan, 1912).

The Economics of Welfare (London: Macmillan, 1920), 2nd ed. 1924. 3rd ed, 1929, 4th ed 1932.

A Study in Public Finance (London: Macmillan, 1928)

Secondary

Collard, D, 'A C Pigou, 1877–1959', in D P O'Brien and J R Presley, eds., *Pioneers of Modern Economics in Britain* (London: Macmillan, 1981)

Robinson, E A G, 'Pigou, Arthur Cecil', *International Encyclopedia of the Social Sciences*, Vol 12 (New York: Macmillan, 1968).

Saltmarsh, J and Wilkinson, P, *Arthur Cecil Pigou, 1877–1959* (Cambridge: Kings College, 1960)

SOCIALISM VERSUS CAPITALISM

SOCIALISM VERSUS CAPITALISM

BY

A. C. PIGOU, M.A.

PROFESSOR OF POLITICAL ECONOMY IN
THE UNIVERSITY OF CAMBRIDGE

MACMILLAN AND CO., LIMITED
ST. MARTIN'S STREET, LONDON
1937

PREFACE

THESE chapters were written to serve as a basis for lectures in the manner of those collected in my *Economics in Practice*. As it turned out, they did not break up into divisions of suitable length, and so in fact were never actually spoken. In tone and structure, however, they are lectures. That is to say, they make no pretence to constitute a learned work, and are addressed, not to experts, but to the general reader. This must be my excuse for ignoring the international aspects of socialism. It is not the business of an academic economist, nor is it within his competence, to stand advocate for or against any political programme. But it is his business, and it should be within his competence, to set out in an orderly way the dominant considerations, so far as they are economic, which are relevant to the argument. On the issues between capitalism and socialism that is what is attempted here. I have to thank Mr. D. H. Robertson and Mr. H. C. A. Gaunt, Headmaster of Malvern College, for very kindly reading these chapters in draft, and suggesting a number of improvements.

A. C. P.

KING'S COLLEGE, CAMBRIDGE, *August* 1937.

v

CONTENTS

vii

CHAPTER I

DEFINITION AND DESCRIPTION

A CAPITALIST *industry* is one in which the material instruments of production are owned or hired by private persons and are operated at their orders with a view to selling at a profit the goods or services that they help to produce. A capitalist *economy*, or capitalist system, is one the *main part* of whose productive resources is engaged in capitalist industries. Substantially this comes to the same thing as the definition offered by Mr. and Mrs. Sidney Webb. "By the term capitalism or the capitalist system, or, as we prefer, the capitalist civilisation, we mean the particular stage in the development of industry and legal institutions in which the bulk of the workers find themselves divorced from the ownership of the instruments of production in such a way as to pass into the position of wage earners, whose subsistence, security and personal freedom seem dependent on the will of a relatively small proportion of the nation; namely, those who own and, through their legal ownership, control the organisation of the land, the machinery and the labour force of the com munity, and do so with the object of making for themselves individual and private gains."[1] This definition is, indeed, formally defective, because it does not recognise that public authorities, while 'owning' the means of production, may hire them out to private persons to operate for profit. If the State owned the coal mines or the railways and treated them in this way, capitalism would be left essentially intact. Indeed, as things are in England, capitalist farmers frequently do not own their land; and it makes no substantial difference to their operations whether the owner is a private landlord or a county council. But these are secondary matters.

Twenty years ago we might have set against these definitions for capitalism two corresponding ones for socialism. A socialised industry is one in which the material instruments of production are owned by a public authority or voluntary association and operated, not with a view to profit by sale to other people, but for the direct service of those whom the authority or association represents. A socialised system is one the *main part* of whose productive resources are engaged in socialised industries. As Mr. and Mrs. Webb wrote in 1923: "The only essential feature in socialisation is that industries and

[1] *The Decay of Capitalist Civilisation*, p. 2.

services, with the instruments of production which they require, should not be 'owned' by individuals and that industrial and social administration should not be organised for the purpose of obtaining private profit".[1]

Since, in these definitions, an essential characteristic of socialisation, as distinguished from capitalism, is the absence of profit, we had best make sure that there is no misunderstanding as to what this means. Clearly it is not the same thing as monetary gain; and to abolish profit is not to abolish monetary gain. Profit is a particular species of monetary gain—monetary gain secured in a particular way. When a person, whether workman, artist, doctor or peasant farmer, sells his services or his product to somebody else, he is not making a profit. To make a profit in the sense here relevant implies performing a middleman's or an entrepreneur's function, hiring the services of other men or buying goods from other men, selling the product of the services or the goods and obtaining as a reward the difference between outlay and receipts. This is what, for the purpose of our definition, making a profit means. To abolish profit is to abolish this—every kind of middleman's service for gain—and, therewith, payment for it.

But, instead of saying that socialism differs

[1] *The Decay of Capitalist Civilisation*, p. 247.

3

from capitalism in excluding profit in the above sense, popular writers often say that it differs from it in excluding the *profit motive*. They contrast "production for profit", meaning *for the sake of* monetary gain, with "production for use". Such language at once introduces prejudice and entails confusion. A private shopkeeper need not be more self-regarding or less altruistic than the manager of a co-operative store. A farmer who pays men to grow bacon for his own table need not act from higher motives than one who pays them to grow beans, sells the beans, and buys bacon with the proceeds. If the "profit motive" is used to signify the motive of personal monetary gain, that motive need not rule when remuneration takes the form of profit; and it may rule when remuneration does not take that form, but appears, for example, as wages, salaries or professional fees. It is, therefore, correct to say, if profit is defined as I have defined it, that to substitute socialism for capitalism would eliminate profit, but incorrect to say that it would eliminate the profit motive. It might or might not lessen the range over which the desire for personal pecuniary gain governs conduct. Whether it would do so or not is an issue of experimental fact. In point of logic it *need* not do so. If misleading implications are to be avoided, the distinction between socialism and capitalism must be made to turn on the absence from the former of the *fact* of profit; and we must not use, as a loose synonym for that, the phrase *profit motive*.[1]

[1] Some opponents of capitalism lay stress on the fact that in present conditions the profit motive plays a larger part in business than it does in professions. This fact is not strictly relevant to the issue between capitalism and socialism, but it is, none the less, a thing to be explained. The effects on other people of what men do in business are less immediately obvious than the effects of what, say, a surgeon does. This remoteness and difficult visibility accounts for the contrast which Mr. Allan emphasises "between Morgan and Harriman battling for the control of a railroad, and thereby bringing on panic, and Morgan and Harriman at worship; between Rockefeller receiving 'drawbacks' and driving competitors remorselessly out of business and Rockefeller picnicing and singing hymns under the trees of Forest Hills with the Sunday-school children of the Euclid Avenue Baptist Church" (*The Lords of Creation*, p. 90). If it were not that the consequences of relentless business policy appear at the Directors' Board, not in their native vesture, but through the monetary ghosts that represent them, inconsistencies so stark could not, it would seem, be entertained. "Even more remote from the directors' conference table than the investor was the labouring man; if mills were closed, or wages were cut, or thugs were hired to break up a protest meeting in the mining-camps, the families upon which the burden of such policy would fall were not easily visualised, as were the boys of one's little club in the slums. They were very far off; the figures on the profit and loss account were very near and very persuasive. When men in Wall Street spoke of Steel, what did they mean? An organisation of over one hundred thousand human beings labouring at desks and in mills and in mines with families to support, rent to pay, food and shoes to buy? Not at all. Steel was the symbol on the pick-up tape; it was a counter in a speculative game; something one bought at 48 and sold at 56, something that the Chicago crowd were bulling, and Standard Oil crowd were gunning for" (*ibid.* pp. 93-4).

5

The definitions that I have given above, alike for a particular socialised industry in a capitalist system and for generalised socialism, would, I think, have been widely accepted twenty years ago. The definition of a particular socialised industry would be accepted still. But, under the influence of the Russian experiment, the definition of general socialism has been modified. Twenty years ago there was little talk of central planning. Socialism entails, it was then held, (1) the extrusion of private profit-making, in the sense of one man or group hiring other men and selling their output for profit to a third party; and (2) the public or collective ownership of the means of production (other than human beings). Neither of these requirements singly make necessary any form of central planning; nor do the two together. Thus the extrusion of profit-making by itself could be accomplished through the organisation of all industries in *independent* consumers' co-operative societies, municipal enterprises and public boards; the choice between these forms being made to suit the special conditions of the several industries. Under such a system the work of managing and marketing would everywhere be done by salaried officials; all capital would be hired at fixed interest; and profit, as defined here, would not exist. The collective or public *ownership* of instruments of

6

production is equally feasible without any associated central planning. If private profit were allowed, the owners could simply hire out their land and other instruments to entrepreneurs; if private profit were not allowed, they could hire them out to co-operative societies and public boards. The fact that there was only one hirer-out of these things would not create a difficulty, any more than does the fact that there is only one seller of monopolised goods. The several hirers would constitute a market of purchasers, the owner fixing whatever price or prices he chose. He might, of course, choose so to fix them that, at the ruling price, there was too much land or too many instruments to meet the demand, so that some were left permanently idle; or, alternatively, so to fix them that there was too little to go round, and distribution among would-be hirers had to be arranged by some kind of rationing. Presumably in practice he would try to fix them in such a way as to clear the market without a surplus and without a deficiency. But, whatever he did in this matter, there would be no necessity for central planning. None the less, at the present day the notion of central planning is commonly introduced into definitions of socialism. Thus Mr. Morrison writes: "The important essentials of socialism are that all the great industries and

7

the land should be publicly or collectively owned, and that they should be conducted (in conformity with a national economic plan) for the common good instead of for private profit".[1] Plainly, if we accept this, the question whether central planning is a necessary incident of general socialism is not open to debate; it is settled by the way in which we have decided to use words.

This does not imply, of course, that a socialist economy and a planned economy are one and the same thing. There are many possible sorts of planned economy. Thus we can imagine a small aristocratic group at the head of a community of slaves, planning the industry of a country exclusively in its own interest without any regard for that of the slaves. Nobody would call this socialism. What is required of socialism is, not simply central planning as such, but planning of a certain character. A planned economy where the end aimed at is obviously and avowedly the advantage of a narrow governing clique is not socialism. According to Mr Morrison the kind of planning implied in socialism is planning "for the common good". This concept may, of course, be interpreted in a variety of ways. In a country victimised or threatened by external aggression planning for the common

[1] *An Easy Outline of Modern Socialism*, p. 9.

8

good might mean concentrating the whole of the country's resources on creating military power. Even apart from war and threats of war, the common good is an elusive concept. How far is it to the common good to sacrifice material well-being in the interest of such imponderables as personal liberty, freedom of association, the sense of a classless society; how, when there is conflict, should the balance be struck between a greater aggregate output of goods, a distribution more even among different people, a distribution more even as between different times; and so on? Can it properly be said that "the common good" is being pursued when particular classes of persons inside the community, the one-time bourgeois, the priests, or the Jews, are singled out for persecution? It is impossible to answer these questions; and, even if it were possible to answer them to one's own satisfaction, it would be absurd to maintain that socialism entails planning for the common good in the particular sense in which we personally interpret that phrase. Planning for the common good must mean, for the present purpose, planning that *is generally believed* in a vague and loose way to be *intended* for the benefit, not of a limited class, but of "the community as a whole". Planning of this sort, in addition to the exclusion of profit-making and the collective or public

9

ownership of the means of production, is now generally held to be among the essential features of socialism.

From the phrasing of our definitions or descriptions it is plain that particular socialised industries may, indeed *must*, exist—witness the armed forces, the Royal Mint, structures such as lighthouses—in a capitalist system. These are islands in the capitalist sea. In the same way particular capitalist industries may exist in a socialised system—lakes in the socialist continent. The primary concern of this book is not with either the islands or the lakes. The main discussion will be focused upon *general* socialism as an alternative to the industrial systems now current in the Western world. Of what has to be said a part will also be relevant to the issue between capitalism and socialism in particular industries. Among the chapters that follow, for example, the fifth, in which I shall consider remuneration by profit in relation to technical efficiency, will be wholly relevant to it. So also will a part of the discussion (in Chapter III) on alternative methods of controlling the distribution of resources among particular industries. But such questions as whether, if the capitalist system as a whole is retained, the peculiar circumstances of certain specified industries, *e.g.* the armaments industry, or the coal industry, make it desirable that they should be socialised, will not be discussed. My theme is a socialist system, not the socialisation of particular industries inside a capitalist system.

CHAPTER II

DISTRIBUTION OF WEALTH AND INCOME AMONG PERSONS

POPULAR discussions of socialism are often preceded by a preliminary attack on the present industrial system. This is chiefly directed against existing inequalities of wealth and income and the serious evils with which they are associated. The attack is powerful and well grounded. The first business of this chapter is to set out in order the relevant facts for Great Britain and to indicate in a general way what they imply.

Let us begin with the distribution of property. Professor Daniels and Mr. Campion have recently published an elaborate inquiry into the distribution of privately owned capital—personal capital—in England and Wales. From their investigation it appears that, for the period 1924–30, the most recent that they were able to study in detail, "1 per cent of the persons aged 25 and over in England and Wales owned 60 per cent of the total [privately owned] capital"; while, at the other extreme, "three-quarters of the total number of persons aged 25 and over owned only 5 per cent of the total capital in 1924–30; and if household goods, furniture and, perhaps, privately owned houses are excluded from this total capital, the percentage was even less than 5 per cent".[1] Of course, when it is said that 1 per cent of persons over 25 own 60 per cent of the total capital, this does not mean that only 1 per cent *benefit from* that proportion of it. If each of these persons was one of a married pair, the other of whom had no property, the percentage of persons over 25 *enjoying* 60 per cent of the total capital would be, not 1 per cent, but 2 per cent. No similar adjustment has to be made for children; they were already allowed for when we made the percentage refer to persons over 25. But it is not necessary to go into refinements. The crude figures amply show, on the one hand, that an enormous proportion of the country's personal capital is concentrated among a very small number of persons; and, on the other hand, that an enormous part of the population own per head an extremely small amount of property.

This large inequality in the ownership of capital carries with it, of course, large inequality in incomes derived from capital, or, perhaps it would be better to say, from property rights. Now we have it on Dr. Bowley's authority that

[1] *The Distribution of National Capital*, 1936, pp. 53-4.

about a third of the total income enjoyed in England and Wales is derived from property rights. Roughly, then, we may conclude that 1 per cent of persons over 25 derive from their property rights not very much less than 20 per cent of the total income of the country. This implies that a small number of persons are in a position, even if they do no work, to draw and to expend very substantial individual incomes. Property rights are so distributed as to make possible the existence of a class of people of "private means" who do not earn anything by work; and we know, as a fact, that this class actually exists.

The class has two divisions. The first contains those persons who, though they earn nothing, or practically nothing, by work, none the less perform work, and that of a very important kind. Many wealthy English landlords have worked extremely hard in the management of their estates. Many rich men have used their wealth in preparing themselves by travel and study for public service, and have lived lives far more laborious than the majority of their fellows. Nobody, for example, without being laughed at, could speak of the Cecil family as idle parasites. Yet, again, besides working hard themselves, a number of rich men have used incomes derived from property for the encouragement of arts and sciences to the great benefit of the world. Witness the Medicis; witness, in a very different field, some of the benefactions of Carnegie and the Rockefeller Institute. No doubt, in an ideal society private benefactions for good causes would not be needed; public authorities would always be on the watch to provide what was required. But, none the less, it is proper, when the evils sometimes associated with large incomes from private property are cited in condemnation of the existing economic order, that the good sometimes associated with them should be cited also.

The second division of the class that lives by owning contains those who not only need do no work, but who in fact do none. It is this group that Professor Tawney in his *Acquisitive Society* scathingly describes. "The *rentier* and his ways, how familiar they were in England before the war. A public school and then club life in Oxford or Cambridge, and then another club in town; London in June when London is pleasant, the moors in August and pheasants in October, Cannes in December and hunting in February and March; and a whole world of rising bourgeoisie eager to imitate them, sedulous to make their expensive watches keep time with this preposterous calendar!" [1] It is not

[1] *Loc. cit.* pp. 37-8.

chiefly on account of the material drain which they make upon the real income of goods and services accruing to the community that the spectacle of this class is repulsive to persons of public spirit. After all, it may be argued, the real income that they consume might not have come into existence at all unless their ancestors, for the purpose of enabling them to consume it, had made special efforts to work and save, and so helped to build up productive equipment. It is the moral, not the economic, evil that repels; the refusal of the dictate *"noblesse oblige"*; the denial of the text "to whom much is given, from him shall much be required"; the enthronement in the public mind of the selfish life as the admirable life; the emblazonment of the motto "I take" in place of the motto "I serve". Professor Tawney's generous indignation will be widely shared. There is not the least doubt that the existence of this group of persons—the product of large incomes from property rights— is a grave social evil, grave in itself, grave because of the false standards that it implants in the minds of would-be imitators, and grave, above all, for the bitter sense of wrong and injustice that it creates among the hardworking poor.

But, of the favoured persons whom the possession of large incomes from property rights relieves from the need to earn income by work, the great bulk do not in fact refrain from doing this. The possession of substantial private means helps them, on the contrary, to secure work of an especially remunerative kind. There are a number of opportunities in business, for example, open to those who can, but not to those who cannot, bring some capital with them. But this is a minor matter. The main thing is that private means, by rendering it unnecessary for their possessor to go to work at 16, make easy the road for education and special training—the long period of learning and preparation that is essential, for example, in such professions as those of medicine and law. The possession of private means, in short, enables capital to be invested in the development of personal capacity, and so creates earning power. Thus the fortunate owners of substantial private means not only possess a source of income in that way, which their less fortunate fellows lack, but also are able to acquire a training and equipment which makes their work, when they undertake it, worth more than other people's. Unequal distribution of incomes from property makes for unequal distribution of incomes as a whole, not only directly through its existence, but also indirectly through its effect on other incomes.

All this has been preliminary to our main

theme, the general distribution of income as a whole. What for this country are the facts about that? From time to time estimates have been made, based, for the larger incomes, upon data published by the Income-tax Commissioners, for the lower incomes upon statistics of wages and other more difficult data. A recent estimate, prepared by Mr. Colin Clark, is set out in the table that follows:

INCOME DISTRIBUTION [1]

Income			Nos. (ooo)	Income (£m.)
Over £10,000 .	.	.	10	221
£2000–10,000 .	.	.	100	378
£1000–2000	.	.	199	237
£500–1000	.	.	508	312
£250–500	.	.	1,527	404
Over £250	.	.	2,344	1,552
£125–250	.	.	4,925	980
Below £125	.	.	11,600	1,170
TOTAL	.	.	18,869	3,702

This table relates to *personal* incomes, not to

[1] The Economic Position of Great Britain, 1936. *London and Cambridge Memorandum*, p. 42. In the total given in the table incomes from War Loan interest are included. This is proper for the present purpose, though, since these incomes are in the nature of transfers, it would not be proper in an estimate of net "social" income.

18

incomes of institutions or public bodies, and it does not include payments made to the unemployed. It will be observed that at the top end of the scale some 12 per cent of the income-receivers took 42 per cent of the whole national income; while at the bottom end some 60 per cent of the income-receivers had less than £125 a year, *i.e.* about £2, 8s. a week. In trying to picture precisely what these figures mean, we meet the same difficulty in a more serious form that was met about capital. The incomes to which the figures relate are incomes accruing to individuals. Of the 60 per cent of income-receivers earning less than £125 a year a number are children or women. What we really want to know is how income is distributed among family households, or, better still, among family households of various sizes and compositions. For households of a given size the thing of primary importance is the amount of the total income, not the question whether it is secured in one large income by the man or in a number of smaller incomes by the man and his wife and, perhaps, two children. But knowledge of the number of individual incomes of different sizes does not enable us to draw up tables describing family incomes. Thus the information we chiefly want is not at present available. Still, Mr. Clark's table at least makes it plain that, for income, as for property, though less markedly, a very large proportion is concentrated on a small proportion of the people; while a large proportion of the people enjoy, alike per individual and per family, very small incomes. The figures that I have quoted refer, of course, to pre-tax incomes, not to incomes as they are left after income tax has been deducted. In this country, as everybody knows, income and surtax are steeply graduated against large incomes, so that the largest are mulcted to the extent of 10s. in the £. Evidently, in view of this, incomes available for use—post-tax incomes—are much less highly concentrated than pre-tax incomes. But, no less evidently, even among post-tax incomes, concentration is high, inequality of distribution large.

The following passage of Mr. Clark's on *National Income and Outlay* throws further light on the matter: "The net effect of taxation and local rates in 1935 can be described as a redistribution of £91 millions from the rich to the poor in the form of services, other than those provided for from the proceeds of working-class taxation. The £685 millions paid by the rich in indirect and direct taxation provides £263 millions of services beneficial to themselves, £91 millions for transfer as above, and the whole cost (£331 millions) of general administration and of public saving not covered by miscellaneous revenue".[1]

The uneven distribution of post-tax available income brings it about that large masses of productive resources are devoted to satisfying the whims of the rich—providing them with expensive motor cars, fine houses, fashionable dresses and so on—while large numbers of people are inadequately fed, clothed, housed and educated. The maldistribution of productive resources as between essential and superfluous *things* is not, of course, as is sometimes loosely supposed, a *further* evil, superimposed upon and additional to the evil of unequal distribution of incomes among persons. It is the same evil viewed from a different angle. But it is, none the less, real and exceedingly important. The reason why widely unequal distribution of income is an evil is that it entails resources being wasted, in the sense that they are used to satisfy less urgent needs while more urgent needs are neglected. Obviously the evil is a very grave one. It is particularly grave in its effects on the young; for, in so far as poverty deprives the children of the poor of proper nutrition and of educational opportunities, it weakens their earning power later on, and so tends to perpetuate itself. Inequality of income in one generation is thus not

[1] *Loc. cit.* p. 148.

merely an evil in itself, it is also a cause of inequality in the next generation. These considerations constitute a powerful case for *some sort* of change making for increased equality; provided always that such a change can be accomplished without entailing new evils as serious as those that are attacked.

What sorts of change then suggest themselves? First, of course, death duties might be graduated still more steeply than they are against large estates. There are also available plans of the type suggested by the Italian economist Rignano for taxing estates that are inherited more severely at the second and later transfers than at the first. An ingenious modification of this plan has been proposed by Dr. Dalton. His scheme is that, when an estate is inherited, there should be levied, besides estate duty in its present form, a second duty, against which the inheritor is given an annuity, to be paid *during his life* and to lapse at his death, roughly equal to the income that would have been yielded by the sum taken under the duty. Measures like these, by reducing inequalities in property ownership, would indirectly reduce inequalities in pre-tax incomes; and this, of course, implies that post-tax incomes also would be rendered less unequal. Secondly, income tax might be graduated more steeply. This would obviously diminish the inequality of post-tax incomes, even though it had no direct effect on pre-tax incomes. But, in so far as large post-tax income facilitates the accumulation of property, which yields further income, the imposition of heavy taxes on rich people would probably also render pre-tax incomes less unequal, and so would affect post-tax incomes in a double way. Thirdly, subsidies, provided out of taxes on better-to-do persons, might be paid to encourage the production of things that enter predominantly into the purchases of the poor. This device for transferring income is an indirect one; but, for some things, such as housing and milk, which are, perhaps, *needed* even more than they are *wanted*, it is effective. Finally, State-provided social services might be greatly extended and improved, with particular regard to the physical and mental development of the young. What is possible in this matter is admirably illustrated in Mr. and Mrs. Sidney Webb's account of Soviet Communism. They speak of the tremendous drive that is being attempted in Russia towards "the re-making of man". In the factories the workers themselves, and not merely the stuff on which they work, are material to be moulded. An enthusiastic development is taking place in health services, medical research and care of infants. There are maternity benefits of a generosity unparalleled elsewhere, and an enormous increase, as servants of the community, in the number of trained doctors. An immense effort too is being made to carry forward and to universalise the education of the young; education is free for all, and all are taught in the same schools irrespective of the position or income of the parents. There has been fostered also a vogue, quite new in Russia, for physical culture and outdoor pursuits; for the development and *widespread use* of museums, theatres and concert halls. If policies on these lines were pressed further in this country—and, of course, there is nothing in the technical structure of capitalism to prevent their being pressed—post-tax incomes would be made more equal by a double process. On the one hand, the benefit received by poor persons under the head of social services would, in effect, represent transfers of available income to them: on the other hand, the improvement in their capacities, to which the social services led, would enable them presently to earn for themselves larger pre-tax and pre-benefit incomes.

In this list of possible remedies for inequality of incomes I have not mentioned socialism; elimination of profit, public ownership of the means of production, all-round central planning. Ought I to have done so? Since advocates of socialism base themselves largely on the evils of inequality, it would seem that I ought; it would seem that socialism must constitute an obvious and direct means of attacking inequality. But here we encounter a paradox. If socialism were introduced by the confiscation from private owners of the means of production, the State would secure at a blow something like a third of the total income of the country, a third which is now, as we have seen, mainly held by rich people; and, whether it decided to retain this income for itself or to redistribute it among the poor, the existing inequality among personal incomes would be greatly reduced. But the official advocates of socialism, at least in this country, do not propose to introduce it by way of confiscation. They propose to purchase the means of production from their present holders at a fair valuation; that is, they propose to hand over to them government scrip, the interest on which, when allowance has been made for diminished risk of loss, will be roughly equivalent to what the private holders are now receiving as income from their property. In other words, apart from minor adjustments, the distribution of income among persons will be exactly the same after the introduction of socialism as it was before. Dr. Dalton, in his book *Practical Socialism for Britain*, tells us this without any ambiguity. "The initial act", he writes, "not being accompanied by any act of confiscation of private property rights, but only by a change in their form, makes no direct contribution to equality." [1] Of course, he does not stop here. He goes on to propose that, after the initial act has been accomplished, vigorous use should be made of fiscal weapons—a steeper graduation of income tax and a reform of the death duties. But these measures, though they are part of the programme of the Labour Party, are certainly not a part of socialism, as, in agreement with Mr. and Mrs. Sidney Webb and Mr. Morrison, it has been defined here. For our immediate purpose, therefore, they are beside the point. The question for us is, not how far would the programme advocated by the Labour Party make incomes less unequal, but how far would the introduction of socialism do this. *Prima facie* the answer is that socialism, introduced as the Labour Party propose to introduce it, would have no effect whatever on the distribution of income. That is our paradox.

But, of course, this *prima facie* impression is only true in part. The act of introducing socialism in the way proposed would not *directly* affect distribution then and there. But the fact of socialism having been *established*

[1] *Loc. cit.* p. 327.

would affect it indirectly and later on. If the compensation paid to expropriated owners was given in the form of terminable annuities, it would clearly do this when the time came for the annuities to lapse. Apart from that, the most obvious way in which it would do it would be through the substitution of salaried managers for private entrepreneurs and of rentiers at fixed interest for ordinary shareholders. For this would mean that henceforward the risks of industry, the chances of loss, with their counterpart, chances of gain, would be shifted from private persons to the general body of the community acting through the State. Under the present organisation of industry unsuccessful venturers lose their money, while successful ones, sometimes through special organising ability, sometimes through skill at outbargaining other people, sometimes through sheer luck, make large gains. Under a socialised form of industry there would be no scope for these gains. The large, occasionally the enormous, incomes, to which they give rise, would no longer be made. To that extent the distribution of wealth and income would be made noticeably less unequal. This is not a small matter. For, as Foxwell once wrote: "It is far more important and far more practicable to take care that the acquisition of new wealth proceeds justly than to redistribute wealth already acquired".[1]

Nor is this all. At first sight it seems that the direct attacks on inequality by highly graduated income tax and death duties, to which I referred just now, are entirely independent of socialism, and could be carried through equally well under the present economic system. But that, socialists rightly claim, is not so. I do not mean that to carry these measures far under the present system would be *politically* impracticable. That contention is not open to socialists, at least to socialists who intend to seek their own ideal by peaceful means. For the vested interests and the inertia arrayed against the reform of capitalism are certainly no stronger than those arrayed against the supplanting of capitalism by socialism. What I mean is something subtler than that. Under the present system a limit is set to the use of these fiscal weapons by the fear that, if they are wielded too strenuously, the accumulation of capital in the country for home use will be checked; since the ability and the willingness of those who now provide a large part of it will both be weakened. As a consequence of this, it is often argued, though, indeed, the rich would be made poorer, total income would be

[1] Introduction to Menger's *Right to the Whole Produce of Labour*, p. cx.

28

reduced in still larger measure, so that the poor, instead of being better off, would in the end themselves be losers. This argument, despite the fact that it is more popular among the rich than among the poor, nevertheless has *some* cogency. Heavy taxes on large incomes *may* to some extent check the accumulation of capital for home use. Even if the proceeds of these taxes are invested by the State and not transferred to the poor, they may indirectly and ultimately do that. Moreover, cogent or not, the argument certainly persuades. It constitutes a real force, under the existing economic organisation, to hold back attacks on inequality of wealth and income by means of fiscal weapons. But, once establish socialism, and the whole argument disappears. The accumulation of capital is cared for directly by the State. There is no longer need to rely on the ability and the willingness of private persons to provide it. They may, of course, be allowed to lend at interest to the government if they wish to do so; and in fact in Russia some of the capital for industry is obtained by voluntary loans. But there is no *need* to rely on these. The State has the power to take whatever it pleases for capital development before any income at all is distributed to individuals. The establishment of general socialism, therefore, both mitigates inequalities of pre-tax incomes to some extent, and also enables measures for equalising post-tax incomes, when pre-tax incomes are given, to be pressed more strongly than is at present practicable. This is so even though the socialist planning authority allows its citizens free choice of occupation, relying on the persuasion of divergent rates of remuneration to secure the numbers that it needs for various kinds of work. If it has recourse to coercion, it has still greater freedom. Without any fear about indirect effects on capital accumulation, it can make, at choice, equal payments to everybody or payments adjusted to family needs. Thus the paradox described on p. 26 is whittled away, and the case for socialism as a remedy for inequalities of distribution among persons is much stronger than, at one stage of our discussion, it seemed to be.

CHAPTER III

THE ALLOCATION OF PRODUCTIVE
RESOURCES

THE preliminary attack on the existing economic
system, by which advocates of socialism pave
the way for their constructive proposals, has a
second objective. In the last chapter we were
concerned with the distribution of wealth and
income among persons; in this we have to do
with the allocation of productive resources
among industries and occupations. This allocation, socialists claim, is exceedingly wasteful and
inefficient. To get rid of the waste and remove
the inefficiency, the blind forces that govern
allocation in Western lands must be set aside
and a system of central planning erected in their
stead.

In considering this charge against the existing
system we must distinguish it carefully from two
others. First, it does not assert that *particular*
industries under the present system are conducted in a wasteful way or are *technically* inefficient. That issue will be examined in Chapter
V. The alleged waste and inefficiency, with

which we have now to do, concern the allocation of resources *among different industries*. Secondly, when socialists affirm that the allocation of resources under capitalism is wasteful and inefficient, they frequently mean that resources are devoted to satisfying the whims of rich people while poor people are standing in dire need. Waste and inefficiency in that sense is not, as I made clear in Chapter II, a further evil additional to the evil of unequally distributed incomes. It is that same evil looked at from a different angle. As such it has already been discussed, and there is nothing further to be said. The charge with which we are concerned now is that under capitalism, when the distribution of income among people is given, the allocation of productive resources among different uses is not "appropriate" to that distribution.

It is not possible to adjudicate on this charge until we have made clear to ourselves what sort of allocation *would be* "appropriate" to the existing distribution of income. This concept of appropriateness is not a simple one. In the present chapter, to help exposition, I shall confine attention to a highly simplified model world. I shall suppose that there are in existence fixed quantities of every sort of productive resource—the various kinds of labour, capital instruments and land—that all of these last forever, so that there is no question of making good wear and tear or depreciation, and that it is physically impossible to increase the quantity of any of them. I shall suppose further that the manufacture and delivery into the hands of consumers of consumption goods—which, in the conditions postulated, are obviously the only goods produced—takes place instantaneously, so that there is no such thing as working capital (goods in process) or liquid capital (finished goods in store). A study of this model will, of course, only take us a little way, and will need presently to be supplemented.

If all money incomes were equal and everybody's tastes and needs were exactly alike, there can be little doubt as to what allocation of productive resources would be "appropriate". Consider a system in which each several sort of resource is allocated in such a way that the last unit of it in any one use yields a physical product of the same money value as the last unit of it in any other use; that is to say, in technical language, a system in which the values of the marginal net products of each sort of resource are everywhere equal. If any *other* form of allocation were adopted, it would be possible, by altering it, to make some units of resources yield a product for which people were ready to pay a larger share of their money income than

33

they are ready to pay for the product that is actually being yielded. All incomes and tastes being similar, this implies that the altered allocation of resources is more keenly desired, and so presumably would yield a larger aggregate of satisfaction, than the original one. It follows that the form of allocation which made the values of marginal net products everywhere equal, would be the one giving maximum aggregate satisfaction, and so would be unambiguously "appropriate".

In actual life, where incomes, tastes and needs are not all alike, it is evident that an allocation of resources on the above principle will not lead to maximum satisfaction; for a £'s worth of satisfaction does not mean the same *amount* of satisfaction to a poor or to a sensitive man as to a rich or to an insensitive one. In other words, the marginal utility of money is different to different people, so that the mere fact of the marginal unit of any type of resource yielding the same value of product in all its uses does not imply that it yields the same amount of satisfaction. It might be thought, indeed, that this type of allocation will yield maximum satisfaction *subject to* money income being distributed as it is in fact distributed; that, so long as no shift in this distribution is made, no shift of allocation could increase aggregate satisfaction. This, however, is not so. Plainly in a community comprising some rich and some poor men a shift of resources from champagne-making to bread-making would increase aggregate satisfaction, even though it entailed resources engaged in bread-making having a lower value of marginal product than those engaged in champagne-making. Hence at first sight it seems that the type of allocation of resources that yields maximum satisfaction in a community of exactly similar men with equal incomes has no special relation to maximum satisfaction in an actual community. Again, however, this is not so. Though it is true that aggregate satisfaction can be increased by departures from this type of allocation in ways deliberately designed to benefit poor people, it is *probable* that departures taken at random, *e.g.* through the operation of monopoly power, would diminish aggregate satisfaction. It is thus "better" to accept this type of allocation than to allow departures from it due to accidental causes. In this limited sense we may rightly call the type of allocation that I have been describing the allocation "appropriate" to the existing distribution of money income, or the *ideal* allocation. The charge against capitalism, which we have to discuss, is that under it resources are allocated in a manner that departs widely from this ideal.

If certain conditions are satisfied, it can be shown without much difficulty that the free play of self-interest in a capitalist régime will *tend* to establish the "ideal" allocation; so that, though friction and ignorance will prevent it from being completely established, the arrangements actually reached will be as good as can reasonably be expected. The required conditions are: (1) that no industry entails costs outside itself or confers benefits for which it does not receive payment, or, in technical language, that marginal private and marginal social costs of production are everywhere identical: (2) that perfect competition prevails everywhere; which implies (*a*) that nobody is able to exercise any degree of monopoly power and (*b*) that there is nothing to be gained from competitive advertisement. The process by which "ideal" allocation will be achieved under capitalism in these conditions is well understood. Each several sort of productive resource moves under the impulse of self-interest from places and occupations where the pay is less to where it is more. Thus it comes about that the hire-price of each sort of resource is the same everywhere. Moreover, from the standpoint of individual entrepreneurs, each of whom only uses a small quantity of any kind of resource, the hire-prices are fixed independently of what he personally does, though, of course, they are not independent of what all entrepreneurs together do. It then pays every entrepreneur in each industry to engage productive resources up to the point at which the demand price for each kind of resource, derived from the demand price for the product, exactly balances the hire-price per unit of the resource. But the hire-price per unit of each kind of resource is the same everywhere. Hence it pays to engage in each industry such a quantity of each kind of resource that the physical product due to the last unit of it there has the same money value as that due to the last unit engaged in every other industry. That is to say, it pays entrepreneurs to allocate productive resources in what I have called the "ideal" manner.

In actual life the conditions set out above are far from being satisfied. In a number of industries employers find it to their advantage to engage an amount of productive resources that is, from the standpoint of "ideal" allocation, too large, because a part of the costs which really belong to their industry is thrown upon outsiders—for example the expense of extra police made necessary by the sale of intoxicating drink. This implies that the cost which they try to balance against demand price is less than the true marginal social cost. Conversely, in some industries employers find it to their advantage to engage too small an amount of productive resources, because, for some of the benefits which their industry confers on the public, it is impracticable, for technical reasons, to charge a fee. This is why the building and operation of lighthouses is never left to private enterprise. Moreover, in some industries a general enlargement of scale leads to external economies: enough machinery is needed there for mass-production methods of making it to be worth while. In these industries the marginal unit of resources engaged by one firm indirectly renders the resources engaged by all other firms more effective. Since the indirect benefits, that are in this way conferred on the public when one firm expands, do not carry with them equivalent extra remuneration to that firm, they do not affect the firm's policy. Consequently, in these industries also too small an amount of productive resources tends to be engaged.

Again, under capitalism resources are misdirected because in certain industries monopoly power is exercised. As everybody knows, such power in modern conditions has a wide range. Wherever it exists the persons in control are able, and it is in their interest, to force up prices above the level that will yield them a normal rate of return. This does not merely mean that they enforce a transfer of income from their customers to themselves. If that were all, the allocation of resources among occupations would be unaffected. It means also that, in order to secure high prices, the monopolist restricts output; which in turn implies that he restricts the quantity of resources *at work* in his industry below the quantity that would be at work there if resources were "ideally" allocated. It follows that the surplus must either be employed in industries in which the value of their marginal yield is less than in the monopolised industry or must be left unemployed. This consequence of monopolisation is familiar and has been widely discussed. I have myself studied it at length in *The Economics of Welfare*. The lapse from the "ideal" allocation of resources that is implied in it entails substantial waste and inefficiency in our present sense.

Yet again, under capitalism, as it actually is in a régime of imperfect competition, a large amount of resources is devoted every year to one or another sort of advertisement. Some of this expenditure serves to *inform* potential buyers of the existence of things that they would like to have; acts in fact, much as the transport system acts, as an instrument for bringing goods where they are wanted. But a large part of it is merely competitive. Smith in effect announces that his product is superior to Brown's and

Brown announces the contrary. The two an-
nouncements cancel each other out, and are
sheer waste, producing jointly no yield whatever, just as expenditure on competing armaments, that leave the relative strength of rival
States unchanged, is sheer waste. Another large
part of expenditure on advertisement—in a wide
sense—is devoted to persuading people to buy
things that they do not really want, or to induce
them to forsake one fashion for another, aban-
doning dresses, for example, that are rendered
démodés by propaganda long before they are
worn out. Much of this expenditure, whose ultimate purpose is to switch about people's tastes
in a purely irrational way, is also sheer waste—
an allocation of productive resources that has no
net yield. These types of waste would not be
present under perfect competition; but in capitalism as it is actually constituted they play a large
part. They entail a further substantial diversion
of productive resources from the "ideal" allocation.

These results are important for the following
reason. Apart from them it is open to opponents
of socialism to argue as follows: "The real
burden of your complaint against the present
economic system is that under it incomes are
grossly unequal, so that the rich divert to their
whims resources which should be used in meet-

ing the vital needs of poor people. This, we grant, is true. But cannot the evil be overcome by directly attacking its source; by carrying further the policy of cutting down large incomes through graduated income tax and death duties, and at the same time increasing, in effect, the incomes of the poor by developing social services, cheapening, by subsidies, poor men's goods, and, maybe, establishing family allowances? If you do these things, the play of self-interest under a capitalist system will impel productive resources into the channels that you wish them to follow—for the furnishing of real needs, not the gratification of whims. Why not be content with this? Why undertake so risky and dubious an operation as the supersession everywhere of private by public ownership of the means of production, the abolition of profit and the introduction of central planning, when what you really want can be secured so much more easily?" Part of the socialist answer to this is that given in Chapter II—that it is not practicable under capitalism to press measures for equalising distribution so far as they can be pressed under socialism. But the contention we have now in view provides also a further answer. On the strength of it, advocates of socialism are able to reply: "Even though we succeeded, by fiscal and other means, in rendering all incomes—allowance being made for family circumstances—exactly equal, we should not by that alone secure that the productive resources of the country were put to the best possible use. The capitalist system would still fail to allocate these resources properly. No doubt, with incomes equalised, the allocation would be much more satisfactory than it is now. But it would still be very much worse than it might and ought to be. By the policy of equalising incomes some part of what is desirable could be attained. But, even so, in a capitalist régime a substantial part of it would be missed. To attain the whole of it there is no way except public ownership of the means of production and central planning". This is the thesis we have now to examine.

Let us consider first failures due to divergencies between what I have called social and private costs. In principle it is plain that these maladjustments are capable, under capitalism, of being set right by an appropriately devised system of bounties and duties—bounties on things whose private cost at the margin exceeds their social cost, duties on things for which at the margin social cost is in excess. But the practical difficulty of determining the right rates of bounty and of duty would be extraordinarily great. The data necessary for a scientific

42

decision are almost wholly lacking. How, for example, are we to ascertain to what extent the social cost, as measured in money, of the marginal unit of beer exceeds the private cost by making necessary the provision of extra policemen; how are we to make the corresponding calculation for a factory industry the smoke of which increases the expenses of the public in washing and cleaning? How, *per contra*, are we to reckon up the indirect benefits that the planting of a forest may have on climate; or that in some industries an increase in the scale of output may have in enabling their organisation to be improved and their average cost, therefore, reduced? Plainly the difficulties are formidable, so formidable that, so far as I know, no attempt has ever been made in a capitalist régime to use bounties and duties for bringing about adjustments of the kind I have been describing. Up to the present suggestions in this matter have been confined to the writings of economists; and even they have never attempted the quantitative study that would be necessary before their suggestions could be applied to practice. All this is true. Maybe, it demonstrates in this field the bankruptcy of capitalism. But what of socialism? A central planning authority would find it no more easy than the government of a capitalist State to obtain the data required for these calculations. Suppose it has successfully fitted supply to demand in some industry under the guidance of çonsumers' offers and its own private costs. It is then in exactly the same position as a capitalist State confronting an industry similarly adjusted. It is no worse, but equally it is no better, placed to improve on that adjustment. For what is needed, in order to improve on it, is not will, but knowledge. The relevant knowledge is of a sort that we do not at present possess, and the eventual winning of which is no more likely under the one system than under the other. While, therefore, it is true that, under capitalism, the allocation of resources among occupations is faulty on account of divergencies between private and social cost, there is serious doubt whether socialism could remedy these faults. Their existence, therefore, under the present system has little bearing on our choice between that system and its rival.

The evil potentialities of monopoly have long been recognized. On account of them nobody seriously doubts that industries in a strong monopolistic position, particularly industries providing the so-called public utilities of transport, water, gas, electricity, and so on, if they are left in private hands, must, in the general interest, be regulated by public authority. Control and regulation are practicable, and are in fact exercised over a wide field at the present time. The maladjustments in the allocation of resources among occupations that monopolisation threatens are thus, under capitalism, held off in some degree. But, experience shows, the control is often weak and ineffective. Hence there is a strong *prima facie* case for extending the range of public *ownership* and public *operation* to industries in which they have not yet been invoked. There is a similar *prima facie* case for extending them to industries in which the wastes associated with competitive advertisement are exceptionally large.

Plainly, however, on this terrain the issue between capitalism and *general* socialism cannot be decided. For in some industries effective control is much easier to exercise than in others. In some countries and under some systems of government control over *any* industry is much easier to exercise than it is in other countries and under other forms of government. There is, indeed, a certain presumption, other things being equal, against the control method. For, if control is to be effective, the controlling authority must possess a detailed acquaintance with, and maintain a minute supervision over, the controlled industries. Would it not obviate expense, overlapping and, above all, friction, if, instead of there being a controlling authority *plus* a controlled one, control and operation were united, as under socialism they would be, in the same hand? *Pro tanto* this consideration provides a valid argument for extending the range of socialisation. But that is not the same thing as substituting for the present system general socialism with all-round central planning.

CHAPTER IV

UNEMPLOYMENT

WE now come to what is, in the view of many competent persons, the most serious evil in capitalist economic systems, revolt against which gives the most powerful impulse towards socialist reconstruction. In a world where there is still a vast amount of poverty and distress the machinery of production is, nevertheless, from time to time slowed down. These periods of slowing down entail a large amount of idleness for machines; and, what is more important, idleness for men and women, who want work and the wages that accompany it, but are unable, through no fault of their own, to find it. Such a situation is violently paradoxical. One set of people are short of goods, another, it may be the same set, are short of work that might produce the goods! Moreover, these shortages are not slight and trivial: they are, on occasions, extremely large. In the depths of the recent great slump, nearly 3 million people in this country out of a total insured population of a little over 12 millions—agriculturists and domestic servants were not insured—were unemployed. Yet again, the shortages are not rare and exceptional events, the consequences of earthquakes or other upheavals of Nature. They are recurrent, more or less regular in incidence, expected and looked for once, or more than once, in every decade. Plainly a system of which these evils are characteristic is open to grave objections. Socialists claim that they are a natural outcome of the working of a profit economy; that so long as capitalism continues, though they may be palliated, they cannot be cured; but that, once socialist central planning is introduced, they will cease to be.

The claim that socialist central planning can abolish unemployment—apart from the short-time frictional unemployment inevitably associated with movements from one job to another—is believed by many people to have been established by the recent experience of Soviet Russia. While in the depression beginning in 1929 capitalist countries suffered from a catastrophic fall in employment, while the official unemployment figures for Great Britain and Germany were respectively about 3 and 6 millions, and the estimated figure for the United States exceeded 13 millions, in Russia there was no *general* shortage of work of the type familiar here, but, on the contrary, a marked shortage of labour. This argument from experience is, however, unconvincing; because during these years the Russian government was engaged in an intensive development of the country under the 1928 Five-year Plan. This entailed an enormous mass of investment in the construction of fixed capital, a state of things that experience shows is always associated with a general boom. Had a capitalist country adopted a similar policy or—what would have had analogous results—become involved in a great war, there can be little doubt that there too unemployment would have been reduced to vanishing-point. For this reason recent happenings in Russia, while they show that, under socialism no less than under capitalism, in periods of abnormally heavy investment there is little unemployment, do not enable us to say that socialism could abolish unemployment in normal times: and, of course, even in Russia nobody proposes that there should never be "normal times", or imagines that successive five-year plans will follow one another in an eternal sequence. This short-cut to the solution of our problem is, therefore, barred, and it is necessary to fall back upon analysis. An adequate discussion would entail nothing less than a full-dress volume on unemployment and is out of the question here. I cannot do more than draw certain distinctions and bring to a focus certain dominant considerations.

We may reasonably postulate that in a thoroughgoing stationary state, where numbers, tastes, technique and the stock of capital equipment stood constant, rates of pay would be so adjusted to productivity that, equally under a capitalist and a socialist system, there would never be any unemployment. Hence such unemployment as there is under either system must be associated with the fact that in actual life conditions are not stationary, but, on the contrary, in perpetual movement. This movement has two principal forms. The first is *relative* movement, such as is originated, for example, when people's tastes shift over from one thing to another, when mines in one district are worked out and those of another opened up in place of them, and so on. The second is *absolute* movement of the kind that is manifest under capitalist systems in those generalised booms and slumps that affect the main body of a country's industry in the same sense and at the same time. Each of these two forms of movement is associated in capitalist systems with unemployment. But, for purposes of a comparison between socialism and capitalism, they have entirely different characteristics.

Relative movements are associated with unemployment partly because all movement occupies time and, during that time, a man in movement is necessarily unemployed. If, for example, every man changed his job once a year and took three days in the process, this would entail an average volume of unemployment of about 1 per cent. But, of course, in actual life men who have been trained to one type of industry cannot, in response to changes in demand, shift quickly to another type; and men who have established their homes in one place are unwilling to shift quickly to another place, even though the work on offer there is the same as the work they have been doing. In so far as this sort of immobility exists, there tend to be established in the several industries and the several centres of the same industry a number of men in excess of the number that, at the current rate of wages, is needed in times of relative depression. Since some industries and some centres are always suffering relative depression, it follows that, unless wages move up and down freely enough to take up the whole slack, there must always be some industries and centres in which some men are unemployed. Unemployment associated with relative movements of taste, technique and so on is not, however, in existing capitalist systems a very important part of the whole. It is, moreover, quite certain that socialism, since

51

it could not prevent movements from industry to industry and from place to place occupying a certain time, could not abolish all of it. For my present purpose, therefore, I shall leave this sort of unemployment out of account and concentrate attention on unemployment associated with those absolute movements that manifest themselves in booms or slumps. It must be remembered, however, that, as between industries that make consumption goods and industries that make capital goods, relative movements occur, not independently, but as parts of these absolute movements.

There is general agreement that absolute movements of industrial activity on a large scale are usually centred in changes of attitude towards investment on the part of persons interested in the manufacture of capital goods. These changes of attitude may be brought about by a variety of causes, some having to do with physical facts, some with psychological states. Decisions to open up new types of enterprise and to exploit inventions or improvements are taken from time to time, as Professor Schumpeter suggests, by a few leading personalities— true entrepreneurs—the urge of whose energy draws others in their train. These decisions are not spread evenly through time, but, for some reason that is imperfectly understood, "appear,

if at all, discontinuously in groups or swarms".[1]
Whatever the nature of the impulse that sets up
expansions or declines in the capital-making
industries, these expansions or declines are
associated in modern capitalist systems with
upward and downward swings in the money income available to the people attached to those
industries. These entail swings in money demand
for the product of other industries, and so set up
expansions or declines there also. Thus upward
and downward movements become generalised.
The movements, primary and secondary alike,
carry with them large swings in the money
demand for labour. Moreover, in the modern
world, especially in this country, money rates of
wages are considerably "sticky", and do not
move readily either up or down. Hence the
swings in money demand affect the volume of
employment, upward swings expanding and
downward swings contracting this volume. It is
a fact and a paradox that, in periods when the
quantity of labour engaged in making capital
goods is increasing, the extra labour wanted
there is not obtained, even in part, by transfers
from industries making consumption goods, but
the quantity of labour engaged in those industries also is increased; and similarly for periods
of contraction. The wider these expansions and

[1] *The Theory of Business Development*, p. 223.

contractions are, the larger obviously is the *average* number of people out of work. About all this there is general agreement, and in what follows I shall take it as established. In the face of it we have to inquire what, if any, grounds there are for believing that socialist central planning would be associated with a smaller average volume of unemployment than capitalistic systems in a similar general situation.

Let us begin by putting out of the way a consideration, which, though suggestive, is not strictly relevant to our problem. If the capitalism with which socialist central planning had to be compared was capitalism of a purely *laissez-faire* type, with the State standing rigidly aside from business, it could easily be shown that, under it, interest in and, therefore, effort towards, keeping in check industrial fluctuations and the resultant unemployment would be much weaker than under the rival system. The argument would run somewhat as follows: If fluctuations in the output of industrial energy meant that at one period hours of labour were 10 per cent longer and at another 10 per cent shorter, or that at one period everybody took rather more or rather longer holidays than at another, they would entail little or no social loss. Cyclical ups and downs of activity would, it may be, be no more objectionable than the normal sequence of day labour and nightly sleep. In fact, as everybody knows, when industrial energy is reduced, the form the reduction assumes is the dismissal into unemployment of large numbers of men. This unemployment is not a holiday; relief from work in this form conveys little satisfaction and does little good. There is, therefore, little to set against the loss of output—of what the men might be producing —that it entails. Thus industrial fluctuations of the type with which the modern world is familiar involve large social waste. If this waste were a cost necessary to the attainment of some more than equivalent advantage, as the waste entailed in movement is a necessary condition of transfer from a less to a more favourable situation, a socialist State, equally with a capitalist one, while doing its best to mitigate individual hardship, must needs accept it. There would be no reason to expect any more strenuous attack on industrial fluctuations and, through them, on unemployment under the one system than under the other. But the facts are not like this. In a *laissez-faire* capitalist state the decisions out of which industrial fluctuations directly spring are made in the main by private persons in control of industry. When any one of them is considering whether to expand his enterprise or to contract it, or to keep it stable, he balances against one another at the margin expected gain and expected cost *to him*. But the social waste involved in the contribution which his decision makes to industrial fluctuations is not a cost *to him*. When he dismisses a workman it makes no difference to his earnings whether the workman finds work elsewhere or is thrown into idleness. Thus the social costs entailed by industrial fluctuations are not weighed up against benefits and accepted as a price, which, for the sake of these benefits, it is worth while to pay. They are simply ignored. Under socialist central planning they would, of course, not be ignored. Recognition of them would create an impulse towards combating unemployment, which under purely *laissez-faire* capitalism would be entirely lacking. As between socialism and purely *laissez-faire* capitalism the issue is thus not in doubt. But in actual life it is not with purely *laissez-faire* capitalism that we have to do. Alongside of private industry there stands the State; and to the State the social waste of unemployment does entail a cost. It entails a pecuniary cost; for unemployed men and their families cannot be allowed to starve; and a substantial part of the burden of supporting them inevitably falls in one way or another upon State funds. It also entails a moral cost and involves a moral obligation, which, in this country at all events, is winning continually wider acknowledgment. In view of this the impulse to combat unemployment may be as strong in some capitalist societies as it would be under socialist central planning. It seems best, therefore, to conduct the inquiry promised on p. 54 upon the assumption that the impulse will be similar under the two systems. If in fact it is stronger under socialism, the conclusions that I shall reach are *pro tanto* reinforced.

This being understood, my programme is as follows. First, I shall focus attention upon the fact that, whereas under capitalism decisions are made at many centres, under centralised socialism all authority in the last resort is unified; and I shall suggest that the fact of unification automatically excludes certain incidents, which, under capitalism, are unfavourable to industrial stability—excludes them, even though under socialism no deliberate attack on instability is made. So far there is no question of overt remedies for industrial fluctuations and, through fluctuations, for unemployment. Secondly, I shall bring under review the two types of "remedy" that have largest current vogue, and shall ask whether, under a unified form of socialist organisation, they can be applied more or less effectively than is practicable under capitalism. Thirdly, I shall say

something of two further types of "remedy",
which it is open to a socialist State to employ.
This analysis will enable us to reach a tentative
conclusion on the general issue.

Under capitalism, while some industries are
completely trustified, in others there is a substantial number of independent producers.
Where this is so, there is a tendency for each
several producer in a given industry, when, for
example, he foresees a rising demand, to attend
insufficiently to the fact that his competitors are
likely also to foresee it. All the producers together in the industry are thus liable to expand
output and employment in good times, and to
contract them in bad times more than they would
do if they were united under a single control. A
similar tendency exists as between industries,
even if these are individually trustified, where
the several trusts are independent. Each trust is
liable to ignore, when prospects are good, the
likelihood that other trusts will also see that they
are good and, by their joint action, will cause
the prices of materials and of labour presently to
rise; and conversely when prospects are bad.
Under general socialism all the producing
centres in the same industry, and also all the
industries, are subject to a common central
authority. Hence, apart altogether from direct
efforts at stabilisation, the data on which action

is based are better co-ordinated, and an important set of miscalculations, which tend to swell the amplitude of fluctuations, and so indirectly the average volume of unemployment, is eliminated. This advantage for employment would emerge automatically out of *any* unified organisation, whether socialist or capitalistic.

Turn to the second line of inquiry distinguished on p. 57. The two types of remedy for unemployment that have the largest vogue may be compendiously summarised as "public works policy" and "monetary policy". The root idea of the former is that the State (together with the local authorities), by varying in an appropriate way the amount of public investment, should offset variations in private investment, and so stabilise, or go some way towards stabilising, investment as a whole. Since it is variations in investment that start and carry with them, in the manner described on p. 52, variations in industrial activity in general, stabilising investment will, it is thought, mean stabilising everything, and so abolishing unemployment, so far as it is a product of industrial fluctuations. The root idea of anti-unemployment monetary policy, as conceived by many of its advocates, is also to operate, this time *via* the rate of interest, or, more properly, the complex of rates of interest— first the short-term rate and later, through that, the long-term rate—on the volume of investment; the idea again being that, if this can be kept fairly stable, industry as a whole will be kept stable also. There is another view of monetary policy, to which reference will be made presently. But, for the moment, we may conveniently confine ourselves to this view of it.

Either of these two policies, if completely and successfully carried through, would abolish absolute (as distinguished from relative) industrial fluctuations, and so the type of unemployment that we are here considering. Ideally, therefore, they are alternative and rival policies, to be weighed against one another by reference to their comparative social costs. In fact, however, neither policy can, by itself, be pressed home. Consider, first, public works policy as I have defined it above. A given addition to public investment does not automatically entail an equal—indeed it need not entail any— addition to aggregate investment. For the resources turned to public investment may simply be drawn from what would have been private investment. What in fact happens to aggregate investment depends largely upon how the complex of rates of interest is affected, and this, in turn, depends in part on the kind of monetary policy that is being pursued by the banking system. Deflationist policy on the part of the

Central Bank might completely defeat an expansionist public works policy. Thus public works policy by itself is restricted in scope and power. Monetary policy is in like case. It too, in actual life, cannot be completely and successfully carried through as an independent policy. In certain circumstances the weapons available to banking systems cannot prevent investment from contracting, unless they are assisted and supplemented by weapons from the armoury of public works. For, though, by offering low discount rates and purchasing securities in the market, the banking system is always able to create purchasing power, it is not always able to secure that that purchasing power shall be used. If business confidence is at the low ebb, the whole of it may be left in idle balances, and so may fail to act upon investment. Thus neither policy is sufficient in itself. But both may have a part to play. Let us consider the capacity of capitalist and socialist States respectively to operate them.

Under capitalism public works policy, as a remedy for industrial fluctuations, and so for unemployment, is subject to a severe handicap. Public investment normally constitutes only a small proportion of total investment. Recently in this country it has been less than a sixth, though in the period prior to 1931, when municipalities were continuously engaged in housing extension, it may have amounted to a third. Moreover, a large part of public investment is not free to be varied in the interests of industrial stability. An urgent armaments programme cannot be held up till an industrial slump is threatened. Nor is this all. Public authority in a country such as England is not unified, but is split up between the central government and a large number of local bodies. The central government cannot enforce a public works policy upon these bodies, but at best can persuade them by financial inducements. The scope of effective action is thus further limited. Finally, a capitalist government, seeking in bad times to increase the field of employment, is debarred from undertaking any work whose product would compete directly with private enterprise. For, if it did so, part of the extra employment that its action created would be offset by a reduction in private employment; and, even in conditions where the offset would be very small, the outcry of vested interests would be very large, and—in a democracy—usually effective. A socialist system unified under a central planning authority is free from these handicaps, and is, therefore, in a substantially stronger position for effectively operating a public works policy.

At first sight it seems that the same thing

is true of monetary policy. But this is not really so. No doubt, in capitalist countries the commercial banks are, in great part, private concerns. But the Central Bank, though sometimes, as, for example, in this country, also a private concern, is in practice always closely linked up with the State. No doubt, a conflict of policy between the Central Bank and the State is possible. But in modern conditions, at all events in this country, it is very unlikely. In the last resort the State could, by legislation, assume control of the Central Bank without upsetting in any way the main structure of the capitalist system. But control of the Central Bank in effect carries with it control of monetary policy. Hence in practice capitalist States are, or at any rate, could readily place themselves, in nearly as strong a position as socialist States for regulating that policy according to their will. In this matter, therefore, while in appearance socialism is better off than capitalism, in practice there is not much to choose between the two.

I come to the third stage of the programme sketched out on p. 57. It will have been noticed that both public works policy and monetary policy, as I have interpreted it so far, aim at stabilising industrial activity, and so employment, as a whole, by stabilising total *investment*. But occasions are bound to arise on which the

cost and inconvenience of keeping total invest
ment stable would be so great that no State,
whether capitalist or socialist, would seriously
attempt it. Under the impulse of a rearmament
programme, or the development of a new large-
scale enterprise, such as a railway system, or a
decision, as under the Russian Five-year Plan,
to erect rapidly a large-scale heavy industry,
total investment is bound to expand to a larger
annual volume than could be permanently
maintained. Moreover, apart from these extreme cases, it is easy to imagine circumstances
in which to make investment stable by deliberate State intervention, when the play of self-
interest would cause it to vary from time to
time, must involve large economic loss. If, for
example, an earthquake desolated a large region,
it would be much more in the social interest to
expand aggregate investment for a short time
in order to make the damage good than to keep
investment stable at the cost of a long delay in
doing this. Plainly on occasions of this kind what
is really required is, not stabilisation of investment, but expansions and contractions in
investment accompanied by compensating contractions and expansions in the industrial activity devoted to consumption. Monetary policy, as
interpreted by some of its advocates,[1] is regarded

[1] Cf. *ante*, p. 60.

as an instrument for accomplishing this directly
—*via* stabilisation of total money income—not
merely, in the manner hitherto supposed, as an
instrument for stabilising investment. In so far
as it can be made an effective instrument for this
purpose, it is available equally to capitalism and
to socialism. There is, however, some doubt as
to how far it *can* be made an effective instrument.
Under capitalism it can, no doubt, at need be
supplemented by budgetary policy, *i.e.* the practice of budgeting for a surplus in good times,
and for a deficit, thus leaving the public with
more money to spend, in depressions. But this,
too, is a roundabout method. Under socialism,
if the planning authority chooses, the way is also
open, whereas under capitalism it is not open, for
direct and indubitably effective action. Having
control of all industries, presumably through
some such system of subordinate bodies as
exists in Russia, it can accompany decisions to
contract activity in capital-making industries
with contemporary decisions to increase it in
industries that make consumption goods; and
vice versa. It can transfer productive resources
for this purpose from the controllers of the one
sort of industry to the controllers of the other
by decree, and not by inducements. In so far,
indeed, as men hitherto engaged in one type of
industry are unable, for want of training, to do

65

the work of another, if the shifts are too large to be met by the adjustment of new recruits, delay is inevitable; and, during the period when the transferees are being re-trained, they will, from the standpoint of industry, be unemployed. The fact of imperfect mobility is thus, as I indicated earlier, always liable, except in a thoroughgoing stationary State, to entail some unemployment. None the less, socialist communities, whose activities are planned from a centre, possess, in this type of direct action, a powerful weapon for combating industrial fluctuations and the unemployment associated with them, that is not available to less highly co-ordinated capitalist societies.

All this is true even if the planning authority allows its rate of money payment to workers to have the sort of "stickiness" or rigidity that rates of money wages have in Great Britain. But, of course, with its wider coercive powers, a socialist State need not allow this. Now, most economists hold that one of the factors responsible for the high average level of unemployment, that this country, for example, has experienced since the war, is the fact that money wages are sticky. For this means that in periods when aggregate money expenditure and, therefore, the general price level is falling, since money wage rates do not fall in equal measure, real wage rates are not merely maintained, but are pushed up. But aggregate money expenditure, as we have seen, usually falls when employers' anticipations of profit from hiring labour are dwindling. At such periods, therefore, if real wage rates do not fall, employment is bound to contract. That real wage rates should actually rise obviously makes things worse. Hence any system that rendered money wage rates more plastic would mitigate fluctuations and so reduce the average volume of unemployment. Some economists deny this upon the ground that, if money wage rates were reduced in bad times, they would cause aggregate expenditure to fall in an equal proportion, and so the last state of employment would be no better than the first. If we do not, as I myself do not, accept this view, it follows that the greater power of a socialist State, as against a capitalist one, to enforce variations in money rates of pay must make it easier for it to control industrial fluctuations, and so unemployment. But, even apart from this, the preceding analysis leaves little doubt that, for tackling the problem of unemployment, a socialist system, with central planning, has definite advantages over a capitalist one.

CHAPTER V

PROFIT AND TECHNICAL EFFICIENCY

In the three preceding chapters I have been considering issues where the attack, so to speak, has come from the socialist side. We have now to shift our viewpoint. In popular discussion the commonest argument against socialisation, whether of a particular industry or in a generalised form, is that remuneration by profit is an essential instrument for insuring technical efficiency, and that any system which endeavoured to dispense with it, whatever other advantages it might claim, would be enormously less productive. This is plainly a very important matter. It is one, moreover, on which we can reasonably hope for some light from experience. In this country, as throughout the Western world, the general system of industry is capitalistic in the sense of the definition I gave in Chapter I. But inside the system, while the main body of industries are capitalistic, some are socialised. There are, therefore, data for comparison. Let us begin by distinguishing the chief varieties of both these main types as they are found in the United Kingdom to-day.

Capitalist industries are for the most part made up either of private businesses (including partnerships), in which liability is unlimited, private joint stock companies of limited liability, and public joint stock companies of limited liability. Whereas a hundred years ago limited liability companies could only be formed with the help of special acts of Parliament, the Act of 1862 removed that restriction; and, since that time, the number and scale of these companies has enormously increased. At the present time neither private nor public companies play any important part in agriculture or the ownership of dwelling-houses. Railways, shipping and other forms of transport are, apart from some municipally owned trams and omnibuses, entirely in the hands of public companies. In industry, retailing, personal services and all other activities the capital engaged is probably shared about equally by public companies on the one hand, and by private businesses and private companies on the other. Excluding railway companies, with a capital of 1100 million, the Board of Trade reported that the number and capital of companies "believed to be carrying on business" in the United Kingdom in 1934 were as follows:

	Number	Capital £m.
Public Companies	14,989	3874
Private Companies	117,075	1721

Mr. Colin Clark has kindly provided me with the following *very rough* analysis, for the United Kingdom at the present time, of capital (excluding National Debt, capital held overseas and non-income-yielding capital such as furniture).

I. Fields in which company capital is unimportant:

	£m.
Agriculture (land and tenants' capital)	1400
Ownership of dwelling-houses .	2000
	3400

II. Fields in which company or municipal ownership is universal:

	£m.
Railways	1100
Shipping	250
Other transport . . .	100
	1450

III. Industry, retailing, services and all other activities:

	£m.
Public companies' capital .	3900
State and municipal capital .	1000
Private companies, and individuals' capital . . .	3850
	8750

Capitalist industries may be further distinguished according to the way in which the parts are related to the whole. In the early days of capitalism the majority of industries were made up of a large number of independent concerns, each responsible for only a small part of the industry's output. Now, besides industries of this type—the Lancashire Cotton industry is a good example—there are others, in which a relatively small number of large concerns are responsible for most of the output. These large concerns are sometimes operated quite independently of one another: sometimes they are bound together on the marketing side by some form of price kartel: sometimes they are bound together more closely, production as well as price policy being unified, by means of a holding company or something analogous to that. Moreover, concerns carrying on successive industrial processes, as well as those engaged in parallel processes, are often brought under a common control. The forms adopted are very various; the choice made among them at any time and in any field of production depending in part upon technical considerations and in part upon considerations of transport and finance.

Of socialised industries there are in this country four principal types. These are, first, consumers' co-operative societies, so far as they supply only members; secondly, municipal undertakings, so far as they supply only the citizens of the towns operating them;[1] thirdly, national concerns run centrally through a government department in the manner of the British Post Office; fourthly, concerns run by special *ad hoc* public boards or commissions, deliberately divorced from direct parliamentary control. Examples of the last form are, the Port of London Authority, the Electricity Commissioners, the British Broadcasting Corporation and a number of others. Under these schemes the controlling authorities are appointed by various groups of persons whose interests are affected. The Port of London Authority, for example, consists of representatives of payers of dues, wharfingers and owners of river craft, and of ten appointed members, of whom two must be representatives of Labour. The London Water Board consists of sixty-six members appointed by the local authorities of the area served. Authorities of this type are required to fix their charges in such a way as to cover interest on

[1] In so far as co-operative societies or municipal undertakings sell supplies to non-members as well as to members, we have in them a mixture of the socialist and capitalist forms. In the main, however, co-operative societies and municipal undertakings supply their own members: just as private concerns and joint stock companies supply people other than themselves. The element of overlap is unimportant and may be left out of account.

capital at a fixed rate, appropriate charges for depreciation and reserve and, it may be, a contribution to the State. In some circumstances it will be necessary, to enable sufficient capital to be raised, for the State to guarantee interest upon it in case the public board's revenue should prove insufficient. When this is necessary, and, maybe, sometimes when it is not, the boards are subjected, in the last resort, though not, of course, for purposes of normal administration, to the authority of a minister of the State. Thus in the Mines Nationalisation Bill drafted in 1919 it was proposed that the State should take over the mines, and that, thereafter, there should be a Minister of Mines, a National Council of ten government nominees and ten men chosen by the Miners' Federation, and a series of district and pit councils. The Sankey scheme was similar, but it gave the workers fewer places. There is, of course, a wide choice among different structural forms under which it is sought to combine socialised public control with freedom from bureaucratic methods, minuting, backward and forward reference, and so on—a form of organisation appropriate to the work of the Civil Service, but not to the control of business.

This slight background of description is enough for my purpose. In going forward to comparison we shall be able, it might be thought, to appeal with confidence to direct evidence. Two such pieces of evidence have been offered from the history of the Great War. But both, I think, must be discarded. First, it has been argued as follows: "If the individualist principle is the right thing, then it was manifestly absurd in war time to do what the government did, for example, in taking over the railways. If divided railway control was efficient, why interfere with it; why not carry on as usual? What was there in the way of moving trains and men that was not the proper business of railway companies? And why, then, were they 'interfered with'? If it becomes obviously necessary to mobilise railways in war to move some hundreds of thousands or millions of men, why is it not necessary to mobilise railways in peace to move to the best advantage nearly 300 million tons of coal in a year—the coal which is the very life-blood of British industry?"[1] This reasoning assumes that the State took over the railways in war time in order to render them technically more efficient. In fact it took them over in order to ensure that the government should have full command over their lines and equipment, and should not have to do without services it needed on account of conflicting claims from private persons. Secondly, an analogous argument has been built up from

[1] Chiozza Money, *The Triumph of Nationalization*, pp. 86-7.

74

the fact that the establishment of national munition factories enabled the government to obtain its supplies enormously more cheaply than it could have done, and was in fact doing, from private firms. But the circumstances of the war were such that the private sellers of munitions, faced with an unlimited government demand, were able to exact prices very greatly in excess of their own cost of production. Such a state of affairs does, indeed, provide a strong argument for national action. But the fact that a national shell-works can produce shells at a less cost than the price that a private works can force the government to pay is no proof that it is technically more efficient. Technical efficiency concerns real costs of production, not sale prices fixed under conditions of shortage or conditions of monopoly.

No less inconclusive are appeals, whether in support of capitalism or of socialism, to comparative costs statistics as between private and municipal enterprise. No doubt, if it could be shown that, *other conditions being the same*, a given output was, in general, obtained at greater or at less real cost under public than under private management, genuine evidence about the relative efficiencies of the two forms of organisation would be obtained. But in actual life this is impracticable. First, the quality of services

75

which are called by the same name varies enormously in different places, and it is almost impossible properly to allow for these variations. Secondly, the conditions of production in different places are entirely different. "To compare a private corporation within the limits of a great city, where an immense supply is furnished, and where special conditions of non-interference with adjoining property rights are to be met, with some municipal plant in a suburban town, upon the basis of the relative amounts of supplies and labour required per unit of electrical energy, would obviously be unfair to both contestants."[1] In short, arguments from statistics, even apart from the pitfalls with which unwary inquirers are confronted in the interpretation of municipal accounts, are, in this field, almost entirely valueless. We are driven back, therefore, to general qualitative analysis.

Before I proceed to this it may be well to clear out of the way a very elementary, but none the less pervasive, fallacy. It is sometimes thought that, in the matter of efficiency, socialisation must have the advantage because profits *in their very nature*, even in conditions of perfect competition, can only be secured at the cost of loss to consumers, and under socialisation there are no profits. This is, of course, not so. Suppose

[1] Bemis, *Municipal Monopolies*, pp. 289-90.

that in two similar countries there are two similar sets of people needing boots and shoes. In the one country the production and sale of these goods is organised through a number of capitalist concerns, in the other through an equal number of consumers' co-operative societies. What difference is there in the output and cost of boots and shoes in the two countries? With competition perfect and no opportunity of monopolistic action, there would be no difference at all. No doubt, the entrepreneurs in the capitalist industry would aim at maximising their own net receipts, while the managers in the socialised industry would be paid fixed salaries and would aim at carrying production to the point where total cost (including those salaries) was equal to total demand price. But in the capitalist industry the pressure of competition would so regulate the size of individual businesses that entrepreneurs there secured the same earnings as men of equal ability acting as managers in other industries; that is to say, the same earnings that in the other country were paid to the managers of the co-operative societies. Moreover, the profit motive would lead the entrepreneurs in the capitalist industry to produce just the same quantity of boots that the managers, seeking to equalise total cost and total demand price, produce in the socialised industry. The only difference, in short, is that in the capitalist industry what the persons in control receive is *called* profits, while in the socialised industry it is called a salary. Apart from this the two systems lead to exactly the same results.[1]

This side-issue disposed of, let us go forward with our main task. Since, as we have seen, there are several varieties alike of capitalist and of socialised forms, some presumably more suitable for some industries and some states of technique than for others, it is impossible to compare the two at large. A more discursive approach is necessary. It is convenient to consider first the claims under this head of the private business—the characteristic form of British capitalism in the days of its youth. When ownership and control are united in a single hand there is greater freedom of action, more scope for initiative, a greater readiness to attempt untried ways and to take risks, a quicker response to changing conditions, probably more drive, than are to be found either in joint stock companies or in any socialised industrial form. Thus the private business form of industry gives scope for people with a little private capital to

[1] It must be remembered that we are supposing the number of co-operative societies and the number of private firms to be equal. To compare a large number of private firms in the one country with a single large co-operative society in the other would be improper.

start some new method or even new product, which experts consider impracticable and yet which may succeed. The late Lord Melchett, in his book on *Industry and Politics*, gives, from one of his speeches in the House of Commons, a very interesting account of his father's career. "It is now nearly fifty years since two young men got to know each other in business. With the very little money they had saved they decided to start a new enterprise. Their capital was very insufficient; their optimism very great. They adopted a process entirely unknown in this country. They asked people who understood the industry to come into it, but they laughed at it. . . . Who would have been prepared to take the risk which all the most experienced men in the industry said was an absurd risk to take? . . . This is only one instance. These two men were my father and the late Sir John Brunner. They did not work 8 hours a day, but 36 hours on end without stopping. They created work for themselves; they created works where thousands of people have been employed. One of the difficulties which I feel with regard to socialism is that I do not see how you can make any progress."[1] For Marshall this was a decisive consideration. He wrote in 1907: "Governmental intrusion into businesses which require

[1] *Loc. cit.* p. 312-3.

ceaseless invention and fertility of resource is a danger to social progress, the more to be feared because it is insidious. It is notorious that, though departments of central and municipal governments employ many thousands of highly paid servants in engineering and other progressive industries, very few inventions of any importance are made by them: and nearly all of those few are the work of men like Sir W. H. Preece who had been thoroughly trained in free enterprise before they entered government service. Government creates scarcely anything. If government control had supplanted that of private enterprise a hundred years ago there is good reason to suppose that our methods of manufacture now would be about as effective as they were fifty years ago, instead of being perhaps four or even six times as efficient as they were then. . . . A government could print a good edition of Shakespeare's works, but it could not get them written. When municipalities boast of their electric light and power works, they remind me of the man who boasted of 'the genius of *my Hamlet*', when he had but printed a new edition of it. The carcase of municipal electric works belongs to the officials; the genius belongs to free enterprise. I am not urging that municipalities should avoid all such undertakings without exception; for, indeed, when a large use of rights of way, especially in public streets, is necessary, it is doubtless generally best to retain the ownership, if not also the management, of the inevitable monopoly in public hands. I am only urging that every new extension of governmental work in branches of production which need ceaseless creation and initiative is to be regarded as *prima facie* anti-social, because it retards the growth of that knowledge and those ideas which are incomparably the most important form of collective wealth."[1]

It is sometimes answered to this line of reasoning that, while, no doubt, the private business form of industry has certain important advantages from the standpoint of sheer technical efficiency, yet, since in fact at the present day the main part of private industry is operated, not by private businesses, but by joint stock companies, this fact has little relevance to a comparison between socialism and capitalism as it actually is. Thus Mr. and Mrs. Webb have written: "In justice to Adam Smith and his immediate followers, it is worth remembering that the efficacy of the process of profit-making was far greater in the first stages of the capitalist system than it is to-day. For a very good reason. Before the rise of joint stock enterprise on a huge scale, still more before the rise of the modern

[1] *Memorials of Alfred Marshall*, pp. 338-9.

amalgamation and trust, the profit-maker was a free agent, a man who called no man master. He was able to act quickly without waiting for the decision of any other mind. If he failed in intelligence or character he had himself alone to thank, and he knew it. If he succeeded, all the profits were his, and all the prestige. He worked day in and day out with this consciousness of the hell of penury on one side, and the paradise of huge possessions on the other. If we think of the life of the modern manager of the joint stock bank or railway company, or the salaried agent of the typical world-wide trust, with his subordination to a board of directors, his obligation to fulfil his prescribed function according to definite rules laid down for him by Company Acts, by auditors' requirements, by the technique of whole series of experts, by arrangements with allied or amalgamated companies; and on the other hand, secured in his salary, and bearing none of the loss of failure, always able to leave one company and go to another, one realises the superior incentive to the brain-worker, and the superior freedom to the entrepreneur, of the period of industrial revolution to that of established and developed capitalism.''[1] In these new conditions it is argued, the comparison that is chiefly relevant is between public operation of

[1] *The Decay of Capitalist Civilisation*, p. 72-3.

industries and, not private business, but joint stock operation, and in *this* comparison public operation has little to fear. For, except for that type of socialisation represented by the British Post Office, where the socialised concern is run directly by a government department—and this type, it is now generally agreed, is only appropriate in rare instances—the structures of a joint stock company and of a socialised concern are very similar. In every case the bulk of the work must be done by salaried officers and technical experts. *Prima facie* it makes little difference whether these are appointed and overlooked by a board of directors, whom shareholders elect, or by a representative committee, or by such a body as the Electricity Commissioners. Moreover, this *prima facie* view is incomplete. It is adequate when the alternative to a socialised form is a single corporation or a closely integrated concern, whose productive policy is under unified control, so that the specialisation of different plants to different uses and the supersession of inferior plants are carried to the limit of economy. But the alternative *may* be some form of price cartel, in which only *market* policy is unified. Arrangements of this kind *may*—not necessarily do—hold back specialisation of plants and keep alive inefficient firms that, under socialisation, would be suppressed. In these conditions the structural form of socialisation is *more* favourable to technical efficiency than that of private enterprise.

But this reasoning, plausible though it sounds, is overdrawn. Two points must be emphasised. First, joint stock companies, as we have seen, include, besides public companies, a large number of private companies, with a capital not far from half as large as that of all public companies, excluding railways. So far as opportunities for personal initiative and so on go, most private companies are, in effect, private businesses. For reasons of technical legal convenience a man, or a small group of men, turn their private business into a private company, and continue to run it just as they have done hitherto. Therefore, broadly speaking, it is not to joint stock companies as a whole, but only to public joint stock companies that the considerations advanced by Mr. and Mrs. Sidney Webb are applicable. Secondly, even in this narrow field, legal structure is not the essential thing. The supersession, where it has taken place, of the private business *form* by the public company *form* does not in logic, and frequently does not in fact, carry with it the supersession of the private business *spirit*. The point is put very clearly by Mr. D. H. Robertson in his *Control of Industry*. "In many cases, while a company

84

differs in legal form from a private business working with a certain amount of borrowed capital, it differs in little else. Sometimes a private firm has reached a stage of growth at which it can usefully employ a great deal of outside capital, which it obtains by becoming a company and issuing to the public debentures or preference shares; while the original owners retain the majority of the ordinary shares in their own hands, thereby reserving to themselves the main prospect of exceptional gain and the greater part of the voting rights. This is the method pursued, for instance, in such large English businesses as Lever Bros. and Self-ridges. Sometimes again, a group of men already rich has bought up in the open market enough shares of an already existing company to secure a predominant interest in its success and an unquestioned control of its manage-ment. Sometimes the promoter or promoters of a new enterprise have themselves acquired a block of shares so large as to give them, if they choose to exercise it, a controlling voice in its affairs." [1] In all these cases the company is both owned and managed oligarchically. In sub-stance, though not in name, it is the private business of one or a few dominating personal-ities. Hence, in spite of the fact that the joint

[1] *Loc. cit.* pp. 75-6.

stock form largely dominates industry to-day, the line of argument developed by the late Lord Melchett and by Marshall has not lost its relevance or its importance. Its flank cannot be turned; it must be faced directly.

Now, it may be that Marshall's judgment is here over-emphatic. He did not live to see, for example, the enormous progress that has been made since the war in aircraft design, largely through government - controlled research. "A hundred years ago, when great overseas markets were being opened up and huge transformations of economic life were ripe for accomplishment as soon as feudal restrictions (Corn Laws and the like) could be shaken off, the business man was not the man of caution, but the man of adventure. The feudal opposition to business men's plans purposed to do nothing at all, but to maintain the existing order of things in the countryside. To-day, however, the business man for the most part is the opponent of changes. Where great and rapid transformations have been accomplished in the last five years, whether in our own country (the grid, the marketing boards, the sugar industry) or in other countries (land reclamation in Italy, the Mussel Shoals Scheme in the United States, the Shannon Scheme in Ireland, the Turk-Sib Railway in Russia), not business men but Governments have been the active promoters. The business man's area has been that of existing economic conditions, which he has wished to see maintained in an orderly permanence. Business men who were not conservative in this wide sense have often turned out to be adventurers in the narrow sense."[1] Marshall, were he alive to-day, might, in the light of these facts, have somewhat modified his verdict. None the less, the line of argument on which he relied still constitutes, within its range, a strong case for capitalism as an engine of technical efficiency in individual industries.

Turn to another consideration. The comparative productive efficiency of the capitalist and the socialist forms often depends upon how far, under the two forms, industries are split up or unified geographically. Thus it may happen that under capitalism the railways of a country are operated by a number of companies; that substantial economies would result from unification; that inability to agree on terms prevents the companies from combining voluntarily, and that the State, in fear of creating too powerful a private monopoly, will not compel them to do so. In these circumstances socialisation on a national scale would, other things being equal, promote efficiency. On the other hand, it may

[1] *Manchester Guardian Commercial*, March 8, 1934. Quoted in J. B. Fisher, *The Clash of Progress and Security*, p. 225-6.

happen that the most economical area over which to organise an electrical power system is smaller than the whole area of the country, but larger than the area covered by most local authorities. In these circumstances there is a danger that under socialisation the industry will be partitioned into sections that are economically too small, whereas under private enterprise proper ones would be chosen. Of course, this *need* not happen; *ad hoc* socialised concerns on an appropriate scale may be specially created; but it *may* happen. The comparative advantages under this head of capitalist and socialist forms cannot, therefore, be determined for particular industries until the detailed character of the alternatives that are practically available are known.

This leads up to a further somewhat similar consideration. In some industries average cost of production will be much the same whether the available productive resources are divided up among few or many productive centres— plants or firms. In others, however, it may well be that there is some size of plant or firm that is more economical, *i.e.* produces at lower average cost, than either larger or smaller ones can do. When conditions of this sort prevail, capitalism provides a machinery by which the optimum size of productive unit tends to establish itself.

For units that are too large or too small find themselves undersold in the market by firms of the right size. Too large firms, therefore, tend to contract and too small firms to expand, on pain of being driven into bankruptcy. This mechanism does not exist under socialism. Some alternative mechanism is, therefore, needed. It is not very difficult to provide this. The Public Board, which, we may presume, controls the industry, can obtain costs statistics from all the plants included in it. On the basis of these statistics it should be able, not merely to discover, and so to get rid of, relatively inefficient managers, but also to obtain a rough idea of what, with a manager of given competence, is the optimum size of individual plant. In this way it can make deliberately those adjustments, which, under capitalism, are accomplished by the blind forces of competition. We have, of course, been supposing that under capitalism the several plants or firms are independent. If they are combined under the control of a single trust, obviously the people at the head of the trust have exactly the same problem to face, and are in exactly the same position, as a Public Board. In this matter, therefore, capitalism and socialism are, it would seem, much on a level.

Up to this point I have spoken as though efficiency were simply a matter of cost, tacitly assuming that, with capitalism and socialism alike, the proper quality of product is assured. Under perfect competition this might perhaps be so. But in actual life competition is not perfect. However true it may be that shady business practices *in the long run* bring a nemesis, the fact remains that in capitalist industries it often pays to sell bad goods. A consumers' association for providing itself with raspberry jam will be under no temptation to manufacture pips for it out of wood; a capitalist jam-maker may do this. A municipal authority will be under no temptation to slaughter animals for food under insanitary conditions to escape the expense of making them sanitary: a private butchering concern may do this. This is a very important matter, so important, indeed, that in industries closely associated with public health it is customary in this country to insist on rigorous inspection, and, when, as in the construction and operation of sewers, that is, for technical reasons, difficult, on public ownership and operation.

There is another kindred fact. Not only in industries connected with public health but in many others affected with a public interest— gas, water, electricity and so on,—it is generally agreed that private operation can only be permitted subject to public control. Nobody would suggest, for example, that railway and gas companies should be free to charge whatever prices for their services they choose. The degree and manner of control vary in different cases, but some degree and manner of it there is bound to be. This implies two things. First, the case for private enterprise, so far as it depends upon the existence under it of free and untrammelled initiative, is weakened. An enterprise that is bound by special State-imposed rules is not a completely free enterprise, and does not necessarily possess in full degree those elements of efficiency that freedom is believed to confer. Secondly, the arrangements for exercising control themselves entail cost, and in strict accountancy this cost, even when it is not passed on to the industry's customers, none the less belongs to the industry and ought to be reckoned as a negative element in measurements of its efficiency.

Since we left Marshall's argument the drift of this discussion has, on the whole, been more favourable than adverse to the claims of socialisation from the standpoint of technical efficiency. But there remains an important consideration on the other side. It is widely held that capitalist industries, even in the joint stock form, are likely to be more efficient than similarly situated socialised industries, because with them bad management may entail bankruptcy and transfer to other hands. Socialised concerns, other than co-operative societies, are sheltered against this. The late Lord Melchett wrote: "What keeps this private capitalist system going? I will tell you. If a private capitalistic business is badly managed, it goes into the bankruptcy court. What does that mean? It means you have a method by which inefficiency is automatically weeded out of your industrial system. You have a method by which efficiency is automatically rewarded. It may be a crude system, it may seem a hard system, but it is the only system in the world which has been devised up to the present."[1] But to argue in this way is to oversimplify the facts. First, in many cases the joint-stock concern, which is the alternative to a socialised concern, would not be subject to competition. A gas, water or tramway system, if it is not operated by a municipality, must, for obvious reasons of economy, be in the hands of a single company. Secondly, even outside the public utility field, many important industries are operated, not by competing companies, but by concerns that co-operate together, sometimes in price cartels, sometimes in closer associations. There is no question of competition here. This consideration, therefore, important as it

---

[1] *Industry and Politics*, p. 317.

is, covers a narrower field than is sometimes supposed.

The general outcome of the foregoing discussion is indecisive. As regards the technical efficiency of particular industries it is impossible to say *in general terms* that the dominant capitalist form—the joint stock company—is superior or inferior to whatever socialised form would be the most likely alternative to it. The comparison must turn on the detailed circumstances of each several case; particularly on whether the joint stock company is in truth a private business in disguise;—and the balance will probably tip sometimes one way, sometimes the other. It follows that the issue between generalized capitalism and generalized socialism cannot be greatly affected—much less settled—by the class of consideration that has been discussed in this chapter.

CHAPTER VI

THE PROBLEM OF INCENTIVE

In the preceding chapter one important element in the technical efficiency of industry was left aside. This is the attitude of mind, and readiness to exercise their faculties to the full, of the manual working staff. When machines are set to work, their performance depends on the will of others, and no problem of incentive or inducement to work, so far as they are concerned, exists. But with human beings the case is quite different. Work by them is not a one-dimensional entity, but has intensity as well as duration. Hence the same number of hours worked by the same people may yield a much larger or a much smaller product according as the surrounding situation leads these people to work at full or at half pressure. Plainly in comparisons between the technical efficiencies of socialist and capitalist economies the incentives to energy that they are able respectively to provide must play an important part.

Under any system except one of dragooned coercion the principles on which wages are regulated largely determine the energy output of the workers, and so the general level of national productivity. Where time wages are paid men are under inducement to work hard enough to avoid immediate dismissal for slackness or incompetence. Moreover, men with a reputation for good work are less likely to lose their jobs in bad times and have a better chance of promotion than they would have without this reputation. Thus a time-wage system does not lack a substantial incentive to hard work. Plainly, however, a piece-wage system, under which more strenuous effort is directly reflected in better pay, provides a more powerful one. The piece-work principle and the time-work principle embody, to put the matter broadly and loosely, the one a large, the other a small appeal to the egoistic motive of immediate personal gain.

Before we consider how far socialism and capitalism respectively are likely to favour the piece-work principle, as against the time-work principle, it is well to make certain that there is no confusion in our thought. To many minds the essential characteristic of the piece-work principle is that it enables a strong and skilful man to earn much more than a weak and clumsy one. This is thought to be "fair"; and the principle is extolled upon that ground. But, in truth, the essence of the piece-work principle is quite other than this. It is concerned, not with the relative earnings of men of different capacities, but with the relative earnings of the same man according as he works more or less effectively. Thus in theory it should be possible to establish the piece-work principle everywhere and at the same time to have the wages actually paid to everyone either the same or adjusted to family needs. This, however, would entail setting up different piece-prices, not merely for men working in different conditions, *e.g.* with new and with obsolete machines, as sometimes happens now, or belonging to different broad categories, *e.g.* bachelors and men with large families, but also for men of different skill or strength working under the same conditions and belonging to the same broad category. Clearly it would be impossible in practice to carry through an arrangement of this kind in anything except an extremely rough way. Substantial inequalities of earnings would inevitably arise under any actual scheme. It follows that, if socialism is taken to include, as an essential ingredient, the rule of equal earnings or of earnings proportioned to needs, the piece-wage principle in fact, though not in pure theory, is incompatible with it. But socialism, as usually conceived, is not strictly tied to this type of rule. While payment according to needs is acclaimed as the ultimate ideal, it is realised that, at the present stage of socialist evolution, to follow that rule would entail an enormous loss of effort and so of output. Thus in Russia the piece-work principle is widely adopted and great stress is laid upon it.

There is a further point to be made in this connection. In industries whose processes are such that individual contributions to output cannot be separately distinguished—in many sorts of agricultural work for example—piece-wages are ruled out by that technical fact. But, under capitalism, in many industries where there is no difficulty of this kind piece-wages are frowned upon by the wage-earners' representatives on the ground that the system may be abused by unscrupulous employers. Where collective bargaining to settle and to supervise the details of the piece-wage system is practicable and is accepted by employers, as, for example, in the English cotton industry, this difficulty does not arise. But it is not always easy to arrange for that sort of collective bargaining; and, if it is not arranged for, the workers often fear that high production will be made an excuse for nibbling or cutting rates; so that ultimately they will find themselves working harder than before the system was introduced and earning no more money. This fear may well prevent the adoption of piece-work practice even in conditions where, suitably safeguarded, it might prove advantageous to everybody. In this matter socialism has an advantage over capitalism. For under it manual workers are less likely to be afraid of exploitation.

The technical efficiency in a wide sense of an industry or group of industries, *i.e.* their capacity for output at a given cost, depends, not only on arrangements about wages, but also, to a large extent, upon the *general* attitude of the manual working staff. This attitude, of course, affects, among other things, the response that they make to the incentive of piece-wages where these are in use; if they are distrustful the response will be small. But it has a wider sweep than this. "The criterion", Professor Tawney writes, "of an effective administration is that it should succeed in enlisting in the conduct of the industry the latent forces of professional pride."[1] The present industrial order, he holds, makes little appeal to this. On the contrary, workers for wages under a private employer or a joint stock company feel that special efforts on their part will merely swell the profit of "the enemy party", against whom they have to bargain. It is difficult for them to look upon themselves as partners in a common enterprise, the success of

[1] *The Acquisitive Society*, p. 184.

which is itself an interest and an end to them. This state of feeling interferes with effective production both negatively by restricting their energies and positively by stimulating industrial disputes which lead to stoppages of work. In both these respects, it is argued, socialised industries have an advantage over capitalist industries.

That claim, so far as this country is concerned, is chiefly based on the unsatisfactory position of the coal industry. It is difficult to know over how large a field it is valid. Against it should be set the widely spread opinion that workpeople engaged on municipal housing enterprises often work less energetically and effectively than similar workpeople in private employment. It may well be that the balance tips one way in the British coal industry, and the other way, say, in these municipal enterprises. But it would be a mistake, in gauging the efficiency of *general* socialism as a stimulus to keen work, to depend too much on experience, or conjecture, about the accomplishments of socialisation in particular industries. For the whole here may be more than the sum of the parts. Thus in Russia there can be no doubt that under the new régime tremendous enthusiasm for work on the part of manual wage-earners has been evoked. Mr. and Mrs. Webb give a vivid picture of the high spirit that these men, feeling themselves servants of their own State, not of private profit-makers, display. They tell, too, of the successful introduction into industry of the *sport motif*, with challenges to beat their output sent from one factory to another—analogous to the tank-week competitions among English towns during the war;— and they describe the development of shock brigades of enthusiasts ready to carry through Herculean labours, not for pay, but for honour and joy of the deed. Here is a remark-able illustration of this spirit of service. "Whilst the huge tractor works in Kharkov were being constructed mountains of rubbish accumulated all around the building; and the inhabitants of the city made it a point of honour to clear it away, without diverting the regular staff from the building and equipping of the new plant, that was so urgently required. Whole crowds assembled on their free days and swarmed around the premises, eventually completing the entire task. On some afternoons, it was reported, it looked like a big holiday excursion getting off the tram-cars, and it is estimated that, from first to last, the participants numbered at least 30,000."[1] This spirit is not, of course, universal. In particular, it does not extend to what the Webbs call "the intermediate class" between

[1] *Soviet Communism*, p. 753.

the intellectual leaders of the community on the one hand and the mass of the workers, mostly recruited very recently from the peasants, on the other—subordinate officials, clerks and shop assistants, stationmasters, and so on.[1] With these people Soviet incentives have hitherto largely failed, and the venality, unpunctuality and inexactness, for which they were notorious in Tzarist times, still remain. But, though not universal, the new spirit is very widely spread. It must, indeed, be remembered that in Russia a new world is in course of being made. It would be rash to expect an equal response when the new order has become established and commonplace. Even then, however, there may well be *some* response. In the matters covered by this chapter socialism should be allotted, I think, some more marks than its rival.

[1] *Soviet Communism*, p. 758.

CHAPTER VII

THE PROBLEM OF ALLOCATING PRODUCTION RESOURCES UNDER SOCIALIST CENTRAL PLANNING

THE broad effect of the discussion so far on a reader who accepts its argument will probably be that the system of socialist central planning, if it could be effectively organised, would be in many respects preferable to our existing capitalist system. But this by no means settles the issue. For the problem of organisation is extremely formidable, and an ideally inferior system that works fairly smoothly may be better on the whole than an ideally superior one whose machinery creaks and groans. This problem of organisation under general socialism calls, therefore, for careful study. We suppose that the authority has decided upon the way in which incomes are to be distributed among people; whether they shall be equal all round, or based on family needs, or based partly on needs and partly on the workers' efficiency. The problem of organisation that remains is twofold. First, how are the various sorts of commodities that are being produced to be distributed among income receivers, when the quantities of these various sorts are given? Secondly, how are the quantities of the various sorts, or, in other words, how is the allocation of resources among the industries that produce the various sorts, to be settled? In studying these problems I shall, to help exposition, confine myself to the same highly simplified model of which use was made in Chapter III. Thus I shall suppose that all instruments of production, including land, last for ever, so that there is no wear and tear and no depreciation to make good; and that no new capital instruments can be made. In these conditions the only commodities produced are consumption goods. I postulate that these are made and delivered to consumers by an instantaneous process, so that there is no working or liquid capital. Yet again—as was done implicitly in Chapter III—I ignore the facts (1) that many sorts of finished commodity are produced, not in a single industry, but in a number of successive stages winding up with the act of retailing them to final consumers; and (2) that a number of commodities are not the result of separable processes, but are jointly produced. To bring these facts into account would make the discussion much more complicated but would not affect the general principles involved. In order then, to attain its ends, what procedures are open to a central planning authority?

The most obvious procedure is to tackle both problems together by direct coercion. The planning authority allocates such and such quantities of labour, instruments and land to work upon different consumption goods, and distributes among its citizens such part of the product of their activities as emerges in the form of these goods. In short, it acts exactly as the head of an isolated farm family might act towards his children and dependants. The work done by everybody, both in amount and in kind, is evoked, not by an offer of reward, but by an order. The amounts of the various sorts of consumption goods that everybody consumes are determined, not by the consumers' free choice, but by government decree. In like manner, there is no free choice of occupation for men in the aggregate. This does not preclude free choice for the great bulk of individuals. The planning authority may well leave most people to select their own occupations, only stepping in to turn away from occupations where numbers are in excess the surplus above the numbers needed, and to coerce those who are turned away into occupations for which free choice provides insufficient men. It may be added that, on the plan I have been describing, there is no need for money, and no purpose would be served by the provision of it. The system is a "real" economy in its purest form.

In studying the implications of this system *let us first take the allocation of resources among different sorts of industries as given*, and consider the distribution of consumption goods among consumers. Clearly the aggregate output, and so the aggregate consumption of each sort of consumption good, is determined by the central plan. This does not, of course, imply that the comparative quantities of bread, boots, and so on that are annually made available are determined without reference to the wishes of consumers, so to speak, in bulk. These wishes will have come into account when the allocation of productive resources was planned. But it does imply that divergencies between the wishes of different individual consumers are disregarded. The quantities of boots, clothes, bread and so on, due to each man, are assigned to him by authority; and he is not free to ask for another pair of boots in lieu, say, of a waistcoat. Moreover, in practice the distribution of consumption goods can only be operated by general rules; so that every individual, or at all events, every member of each of a few clearly demarcated categories *e.g.* single men, married men with three children and so on, receives a similarly constituted packet of goods. Now, if the comparative tastes for different things of all these persons were exactly alike, this would be the best possible arrangement. In a very poor community, where the only consumption goods available are primitive foods and clothes and shelter, the comparative tastes in respect of these things of different people will in fact be nearly alike. But, with greater wealth and the opportunity for a certain amount of semi-luxury consumption, they are bound to diverge. In that event this form of central planning is seriously defective from the standpoint of general economic welfare. One man gets a surfeit of boots and an insufficient ration of bread; another is in opposite case. Errors in the initial distribution can, indeed, be corrected in some degree by subsequent exchanges. Suppose that A and B have each been given one pair of boots and one waistcoat. If A would prefer two pairs of boots, and B two waistcoats, they can make a mutually satisfactory exchange. But the scope of these acts of barter is very narrow. Individuals whose reciprocal desires fit into one another will seldom meet, and three-cornered or more roundabout exchanges will rarely be practicable. Hence this corrective process cannot do much towards making good the deficiencies of the central plan.

But there is a second and alternative form of planning technique, which meets this difficulty. The allocation of resources among different industries still being taken as given, the planning authority may hand out to its citizens every week, not packets of assorted goods, but sums of money. The recipients are forbidden to hoard the money—this rule could be enforced by issuing it in the form of tickets which become valueless if not used within a short time after issue—but are free to distribute it as they please among consumption goods. In order that everything which is produced may be disposed of, the sum of the quantities multiplied by the price of each several consumption good must, for every income period, be equal to aggregate money income. This condition is not sufficient to determine what the system of prices shall be; there are an infinite number of systems that would satisfy it. Among these, however, there must be one system that not only entails the market being cleared, but also insures there being no demand for any commodity, which, at the price set for it, is unsatisfied. It is certain, of course, that the planning authority at its first essay will not hit on a scheme of prices that accomplishes this. There are bound to be numerous unsatisfied demands, perhaps manifested in queues. The existence of these should, in principle, be ascertainable by the planning authority. It can then put up the prices of the things for which there has been a shortage relatively to the original price, and put down the prices of other things. By this procedure, provided that it obeys the rule "sum of quantities multiplied by price of all consumption goods equals money income", it should eventually reach a situation in which there are no shortages and no surpluses. When this is achieved, the distribution of the various sorts of consumption goods—the total output of each being given— will conform with individual consumers' desires. The defect that was found in the plan described on pp. 105-6 is thus, on this revised plan, successfully removed. In principle this can be done. In practice, of course, the task of doing it would be very difficult; and, if the comparative tastes of different people fluctuated, a considerable time-lag in the adjusting process would be inevitable.

Having started with a planning system under which both productive resources and the output of consumption goods resulting from them were allocated by order, we have found that, if coercive assignment of money incomes were substituted for coercive assignment of packets of consumption goods, and if a system of prices of the kind that I have described were introduced, economic welfare would be substantially advanced. But nothing has yet been said about the principles on which productive resources are to be allocated among different industries. That allocation, which has so far been taken as given, has now to be investigated. Plainly no planning authority would rely in this matter on mere accident or mere caprice. It must adopt some principle. If it were omniscient, it would, no doubt, attempt to secure that allocation of resources which I called in Chapter III the "ideal" allocation. We saw, however, in that chapter that the "ideal" allocation can only be secured if differences between marginal private and marginal social costs can be calculated and allowed for, and that the data necessary for doing that are, and for a long time yet are likely to be, lacking. As a practical policy, therefore, the nearest approach to the "ideal" allocation— the distribution of money incomes being given —that the planning authority can hope for is an allocation proper to conditions of perfect competition, with no monopoly and no competitive advertisement, but not corrected, except possibly in a few special instances, to allow for divergencies between marginal private and marginal social costs. But the condition for equilibrium under perfect competition is that in every industry output is such that marginal private cost is equal to average cost, and that average cost is equal to demand price; which entails that the whole output is marketed for a total selling price exactly covering the total costs. Assuming that this is the type of allocation at which the planning authority aims, we have to inquire how far and by what devices it can contrive to attain it. Should it in fact aim at some other type of allocation, the general character of the practical problem will, nevertheless, be similar; so that the discussion that follows could be adjusted to those conditions without fundamental change. The practical problem is so complex that a full discussion of it is not feasible here. I shall, therefore, for simplicity, leave out of account the fact that a socialist planning authority is sure to allow some measure of variations among incomes—adjustments to family needs and so on —and shall proceed on the assumption that it aims at securing equal incomes for all workers. This assumption enables the essential issues to be set out in a relatively simple form.

With this understanding let us suppose, first, that all workers are exactly alike; that equal sums of money are paid out as income every week to all workers; and, further, paradox though it be, that there are no productive resources other than these workers. The workers, let us imagine, have been allocated among different industries in accordance with some rough guess on the part of the planning authority as to what is likely to be suitable. This allocation has determined the output of the several sorts of consumption goods, and prices have been fixed for them in the way described a little while ago. Data are then available, with the aid of which the planning authority can, if it chooses, correct its original allocation of labour in such a way as to convert it into the allocation proper to perfect competition—what I shall call henceforward the *chosen* allocation of resources. For what are the facts confronting it? With a given price system coupled with the original allocation of resources, in some industries what is paid out in wages will exceed, in others it will fall short of the sales proceeds of the product. The planning authority must then diminish the quantity of labour in the former class of industries and increase it in the latter class. It must go on doing this until, in every industry, aggregate costs and aggregate sales value of product coincide. The test is an easy one for the authority to operate, because it can be applied in each plant in every industry by an order to the immediate controller of that plant. Every plant is instructed to take on less or more labour according as the aggregate cost of its product exceeds or falls short of its sales receipts at the established prices. Even so, however, the final adjustment cannot be realised at a single stride. For a shift in the distribution of labour entails, if the principles set out on p. 107 are to be maintained, an alteration in the system of prices charged for different consumption goods. Hence there is need for a series of tentative steps. The goal is reached when in each industry two conditions—not only one as on p. 107—are satisfied; namely (1) that there is no shortage or surplus of product in any industry, (2) that in every industry aggregate costs of production are equal to aggregate sales proceeds. When the planning authority's orders to this effect have been everywhere obeyed, an allocation of resources identical with the *chosen* allocation will have been obtained. There is nothing in principle to prevent the orders from being everywhere obeyed. But, of course, much friction will need to be overcome.

More serious difficulties are introduced when account is taken of the fact that different workers possess different kinds of capacity. To work out this problem, I shall ignore differences in *degrees* of capacity. On the other hand, since no further complication is introduced, I shall now no longer assume that there are no factors of production other than labour, but shall recognise the existence, alongside of labour, of various types of instruments of production. The problem with which we are confronted is now no longer that of allocating among different industries men of a single type, but men and instruments of a number of different types. Under capitalism with perfect competition, from the standpoint of the man at the head of each plant in an industry, the hire-prices of the factors of production—labour, instruments and land—are given independently of what he personally does; though, they are not given independently of what he and his colleagues in all industries collectively do. With these hire-prices as data, the head of each plant then engages that number of units of each sort of factor which minimises his average costs of production, *i.e.* that number which makes the value of the marginal net product, *i.e.* of the difference made to total product by one (small) unit of each factor, equal to the hire-price of one small unit of that factor. Under socialist central planning, however, when equal incomes are paid to all workers, in spite of their being of divers qualities and capacities, and when instruments are owned by the State and not hired out to anyone, there are no hire-prices for factors given by the play of the market, and thus available as data on which the heads of the several plants can be instructed to work. Plainly, if a planning authority is to make the actual allocation of labour and other factors agree with the *chosen* allocation, it must somehow make good this deficiency. To this end it must assign by decree to each sort of labour and instrument what we may call an *accounting wage* or accounting rent; and then instruct the heads of the plants to behave as though these accounting wages or rents were actual wages or rents, so arranging the quantities of the different factors engaged by them as to minimise average *accounting cost*. If and when it succeeds in establishing the correct accounting wages and rents, *i.e.* accounting wages for men and rents for instruments equal to what actual wages and rents under capitalism with perfect competition would be, its problem is solved. But how is it to establish correct accounting wages and rents? A clear-cut test is available. The accounting wage or rent is "correct" if, and only if, at that wage or rent the aggregate demand of the several industries, each acting on the rule to minimise average (accounting) costs of production, exactly absorbs, with no surplus and no shortage, the available supply of every sort of labour and instrument. We can imagine then some such procedure as this. The central authority fixes initially by guess-work some accounting wage or rent per unit for each sort of labour and instrument, subject, of course, to the condition that the sum of these wages and rents multiplied by the quantities of the several

sorts of men and instruments is equal to the
money income actually handed over to workers.
Each industry is then required, as on p. 112, to
vary its output in such wise that (1) there is no
shortage or surplus of product, (2) total selling
receipts are equal to total costs on the basis of
the accounting wages and rents; and also each
individual plant in each industry is put under
pressure to make its average accounting cost a
minimum. When these orders have been everywhere carried out, the central authority will
almost certainly find that the total quantity of
each sort of labour or instrument indented for is
either larger or smaller than the quantity available. It must, therefore, itself vary the accounting wages and rents of the several sorts until
there is no shortage and no surplus of any sort
of labour or instrument. At the same time, in
accordance with our previous argument, it has
to vary the prices set for each several sort of
consumption good so that for it too the market is
exactly cleared, with neither shortage nor surplus; and to maintain equality between the total
selling prices of all consumption goods and
total income. Finally, it must, of course, keep
total income and the sum of the accounting
wages and rents multiplied by the quantity of
each factor equal to one another. It is possible
in theory, through repeated shuffling movements

in accordance with these rules, for the *chosen* allocation of resources to be finally attained. Evidently, however, the practical difficulty of working such a process will be enormous— much greater than in the simpler cases discussed in the preceding paragraph. Far-reaching errors are almost inevitable.

Even yet, however, our difficulties are not at an end. So far we have tacitly assumed that the total quantities of the several sorts of labour are given, so to speak, by act of God. In fact, of course, this is not so. The several sorts are in great part manufactured by expenditure on their training. Let us suppose here, to make the argument easy, that (1) initially, apart from training, all men are alike, with the same comparative aptitudes for different kinds of training, and (2) all kinds of training are equally expensive and occupy an equal time.[1] To bring about the *chosen* allocation of resources a single accounting wage must be fixed for all types of worker, and the planning authority must regulate the numbers to whom the different kinds of training are given in such a way that, at that accounting wage, when the several industries act in accordance with our rules, the market for each kind is exactly cleared, with neither shortage nor sur-

[1] These assumptions enable us to evade questions about the rate of interest, which are left over till the next chapter.

plus. This act of regulation constitutes a further problem, in the handling of which large error is inevitable.

In real life the difficulty is still further accentuated. For different men are not initially all alike, but possess different natural capacities, some being better fitted for one kind of training, others for another kind. The best arrangement would be one under which the different capacities were so distributed among kinds of training that no cross movement of men could increase aggregate output. This arrangement *tends*, under capitalism with perfect competition, to be brought about, because a round man is worth, and will be paid, more in a round hole than in a square one, and tries, under the impulse of self-interest, to go where he will get the best pay. Under socialist central planning this self-selection of workers for different sorts of training is ruled out. The planning authority, through one or another of its organs, does the selecting. When it has decided, for example, that so many doctors are required, it chooses the youths to be trained for doctoring. In so doing it has, indeed, guidance from the State teachers in the schools, and is not groping blindly in the dark. None the less, mistakes are bound to be numerous. The task of selection thus piles up still further the immense burden, which already, apart from this, a central planning authority would have to bear.

The foregoing discussion shows that the practical task of securing that the actual allocation of productive resources shall conform to the *chosen* allocation, can, *in principle*, be solved. But it also shows that the task is extraordinarily difficult. It must be remembered, moreover, that the preceding analysis has had to do with an artificial and highly simplified model. What has been said fails, and necessarily fails, to give an adequate impression of the immense multiplicity of adjustments that, in the actual world, would be called for. Among other things, we have expressly ignored the fact that many finished consumption goods are produced, not at one blow, but in a series of stages, that bring into relation many different raw materials and semi-manufactured products, which in turn enter, not merely into one, but into a great number of different finished consumption goods. These facts do not affect our conclusion that the problem of adjustment is *in principle* capable of solution. But obviously they enhance enormously the practical difficulty. To solve a small number of simultaneous equations in a short time is one thing; to solve thousands and thousands of them is quite another. This is substantially the difference between the problem

that our model analysis suggests and the analogous problem as it would present itself in
actual life. Yet again, it must be remembered,
our model was, so to speak, a self-contained one,
not connected with any outside world. In real
life a socialist State would stand as one among a
number of other States, some perhaps socialist,
others, we must suppose, capitalist. Some of the
consumption goods that its people needed would
presumably be obtained, not by direct home
manufacture, but by way of exchange with
products made in these other States. Here is a
further source of complication—complication
made all the greater if conditions of production
and conditions of demand in these other States
are liable, as they might well be, to large and
frequent variations. In view of all this, it is not
difficult to see that the practical task before a
central planning authority, seeking what I have
called the *chosen* allocation of productive resources, would be one of quite appalling difficulty, and one in which complete success is
altogether out of the question. How nearly complete success will be approached depends, of
course, on the degree of skill and probity of the
controlling authority itself, and of the subordinate bodies through which it works. But, except
in a world of supermen, many and grave lapses
are certain to occur. In any country where

socialism as an ideal is being weighed against capitalism as a fact, this truth must be borne in mind. *Pro tanto*, it constitutes an argument against change.

The preceding discussion will have seriously failed of its purpose if anybody at this point, retorts: "The allocation of resources which you have called the *chosen* allocation is not in fact the one at which a socialist central plan would aim. When a man does not wish to journey to the moon, it is idle to explain to him the difficulties, which, if he did, he would meet with on the way." The stress of this chapter has not been on the precise character of the aim which a socialist planning authority will set before itself. Its purpose rather has been, by focusing attention on a particular aim, to *illustrate* the class of difficulty which the authority is bound to meet with, *whatever* the precise character of its aim. The problem, in short, on which I have been trying to throw a little light, is not a problem of ends, but a problem of technique.

CHAPTER VIII

PROBLEMS CONNECTED WITH RATES OF INTEREST

ALIKE in Chapter III and in the last chapter the discussion was focused, not on the actual world, but on an artificial model, in which (1) all instruments of production last for ever, (2) it is physically impossible to produce any new ones, and (3) all consumption goods are produced and delivered to consumers instantaneously, so that there is no place for working or liquid capital. By this means we were able to avoid saying anything about rates of interest. The time has now come to face the difficulties that surround that concept.

There is a preliminary point about which it is essential to be clear. As we saw in Chapter IV, control and manipulation by the banking system of the complex of rates of interest can be used to modify the amount of employment or, more generally, the aggregate amount of the country's productive resources that are actually engaged in work. Thus, with certain sorts of banking policy, the aggregate quantities of resources at work under capitalism and socialism respectively might on occasions, or even always, be different. That possibility has already been examined in Chapter IV, and we are not now concerned with it. For the purposes of the present chapter the aggregate quantities of resources at work must be assumed to be always the same under the two systems. This condition is most easily satisfied if we suppose both the systems to be associated with a monetary policy in some sense "neutral"—whether this be taken to mean a policy under which aggregate money income is held constant or the "general level of prices" is held constant. It is impossible to enter here into the complicated and controversial issues which these phrases suggest. The broad idea is that, in what has now to be said, we are concerned to study rates of interest, so to speak, in their natural state, not as doctored by monetary inflations or deflations.

With this proviso, the part played under capitalism by the rate of interest—I shall henceforward use this term to *represent* the complex of various rates charged on different types of loan—is easily defined. On the one hand, it helps to determine how much of those resources that are engaged in covering depreciation of capital assets and in making net additions to capital (net investment) are turned into different sorts of capital goods. On the other hand, it helps to determine how much productive resources in the aggregate are devoted to covering depreciation and making additions to capital and how much to making consumption goods.

The careful reader will probably have noticed that there is an awkwardness here. With customary definitions of income, the real income of any year is taken to be the output of goods and services after provision has been made for wear and tear and depreciation. Money income (in the absence of net investment or disinvestment) is *both* the money value of the consumption goods plus net additions to capital produced and *also* the earnings of all factors of production (including those engaged in the maintenance of existing capital); the two quantities being made coincident by the fact that the maintenance charges are included in the cost of production, and so in the price, of consumption goods. Thus it is not correct to speak of any part of money income being expended on making good wear and tear and depreciation. But this does not, of course, mean that no real resources—labour and instruments—are devoted to that purpose; nor does it reduce to nullity the problem of allocating them as between different sorts of capital goods. For, even though no net investment or disinvestment is taking place, but the stock of capital as a whole is being maintained exactly intact, it is not necessary for the stock of each several sort of capital goods to be so maintained. On the contrary, a depletion of one sort may be balanced against an accretion to another sort. Thus the problem of allocation is essentially the same for productive resources engaged in maintaining existing capital as for those engaged in making new net investment.

When this is understood, the way in which under capitalism the rate of interest serves as a link in the chain determining the allocation of those productive resources that are reserved for capital maintenance and net investment is easily described. In Chapters III and VII we assumed that all productive resources yield their final products to consumers instantaneously. In fact the products of resources engaged in different industries, whether these manufacture consumption goods or capital instruments, are yielded, some immediately, some after a short delay, some after a long delay. The rate of interest constitutes, from the standpoint of entrepreneurs, an element of cost, the amount of which, when the rate is given, depends directly on the length of the interval between the use of the productive resources and the sale of the final product directly or indirectly yielded by them. With instruments of production, of course, the final product is not yielded and sold all at once, but continuously throughout the life of the instrument. In effect, then, the existence of a rate of interest discourages the use of resources for distant as against near returns, and discourages it more seriously the higher the rate is. On the basis of the rate the present value of any future return or series of returns can be calculated. Resources reserved for capital maintenance and net investment, so far as their use is governed by ordinary business motives, tend to be allocated in such a way that the present value of the returns on the marginal £'s worth devoted to any one sort of investment or maintenance is the same as that of the marginal £'s worth devoted to any other sort. Further, the amount of resources reserved for maintenance and investment being given, the rate of interest, as settled by the market, will be such that this amount is exactly absorbed by the demand, without surplus or deficit. Under socialist central planning the planning authority, as regards making forecasts of yields, is in the same position as entrepreneurs under capitalism. But there is no market, in which a rate of interest is constituted, to play the part that it plays under capitalism. There is thus no instrument, provided, so to speak, by Nature, through which the resources set aside for maintenance of capital and net investment are allocated among different activities, whose yields are looked for at different future dates, in such a way that exactly all of them are absorbed.

Now there are important sorts of capital goods which are not instruments of production yielding a stream of output, and, through that, of money income. For the allocation of resources to these, under capitalism and central planning alike, the rate of interest gives no direct guidance. What is to go to them can only be decided by a rough common-sense judgment founded on a broad qualitative "feel" for the situation as a whole; the gauge of the rate of interest only coming into play for that part of maintenance and net investment that is left over after these things have been provided. In this class of capital goods fall battleships and roads and—what is extremely important—aggregate investment in the health and education of the people. Here the central planning authority of a socialist State is no worse off than the relevant authorities under capitalism. Nor must another very important species of allocation, to which the rate of interest has no direct relevance, be forgotten—the allocation of education and training among different individuals. Under current forms of capitalism a large part of these sorts of investment is made, and the amount of it decided upon, by parents.

But parents are of very different degrees of wealth; and there is no presumption that the children who would benefit most from expensive education will be born to rich parents. When they are born to poor parents, despite the ladder of scholarships provided, for example, in England, for the fortunate few, they will be debarred from the types of education, which, from a general social point of view, they ought to have. Here socialism has a great advantage over capitalism. For under it, as, for example, in Russia, the State chooses the persons to whom higher forms of education are to be given on the advice of teachers and others in a position to judge their capacity; and nobody is debarred from vocations for which training is costly by the fact that his parents are poor.

Besides these types of maintenance and investment, there is, however, a wide range, over which, under capitalism, the rate of interest, as constituted by the market, plays an essential part in the way described on p. 125, in the work of allocation. Nobody suggests, indeed, that under socialist central planning, in the absence of such a rate, or of some device to take the place of it, allocation cannot be made at all. Of course, it *can* be made—by guess work, by luck, by serving the separate industries that seek capital in the order of their application for it, and in many another way; but it cannot be made in the way that people individually would choose if their choice were left free. *Prima facie*, as between sorts of maintenance and net investment whose products meet the needs of people of similar wealth, this entails a loss. In this sense, a planning authority, unless it can get help from some special device, is practically certain to "waste" resources. It will direct too much of them into some fields and too little into others. In particular, it is likely to be misled by the glamour of spectacular modernity. Thus Professor von Hayek writes: "We should expect to find over-development of some industries at a cost which was not justified by the importance of their increased output, and to see unchecked the ambition of the engineer to apply the latest developments made elsewhere, without considering whether they were economically suited in the situation".[1] In short, over a substantial part of the field, the lack of a rate of interest fixed by the market must seriously handicap a central planning authority in allocating whatever amount of productive resources it has decided to devote to capital maintenance and net investment.

There is, however, a device by which it can meet this difficulty. It is free to construct for

[1] *Collective Economic Planning*, p. 204.

itself an *accounting rate* of interest on the same pattern as the accounting rates of wages and rents that I described in the previous chapter; and, subject to intervention by itself in particular cases, to instruct the persons in immediate control of its several industries to use this accounting rate as a guide to action in the same way that privately controlled industry under capitalism uses the actual rate. The accounting rate must be that rate at which the various industries, acting in accordance with the rules already described, will exactly clear the market, without shortage or surplus, of that part of money income that is on offer for net investment—after, of course, the State has already taken away such part of the available sum as *it* has decided to invest, *e.g.* in armaments and so on, without reference to the rate of interest. With an accounting rate of interest thus arranged the planning authority can place itself, for this species of allocation, in as good a position as capitalism. The difficulty is that, except by a miracle, the accounting rate on which it decides in the first instance is certain to be either too low, in the sense that, at that rate, there are not enough resources available for net investment to fill all demands, so that some are unsatisfied, and the selection of those to suffer this fate is purely haphazard, or too high, in the sense that there are some resources seeking employment, which, at this rate, no industry will take. The solution is to be found in a series of step by step adjustments, accompanied by secondary related adjustments in the manner described on p. 115. By this process the planning authority may hope eventually, if conditions become stable, to find the correct accounting rate of interest, that is to say, a rate which is neither too low nor too high in the above sense. But where prospects and expectations are undergoing rapid change there are bound to be large errors.

So much for the allocation among industries of those resources which are reserved for capital maintenance and net investment. As was pointed out on p. 123, the rate of interest serves *also* under capitalism to determine how much of the aggregate productive resources wielded by the community *will* be reserved for these uses. It does this, granted the assumptions set out on p. 122, by acting on people's willingness to save, *i.e.* to refrain from using income for purposes of immediate consumption. It is not, of course, itself an ultimate cause, but rather an instrument through which the ultimate causes act. The ultimate causes are the openings for investment that are available, or, more strictly, the public's attitude of mind towards those openings,[1] and the rate at which they discount future satisfactions. Under capitalism these forces—forces of demand and supply—determine, *through* the rate of interest, how much capital maintenance and net investment there shall be. Under socialist central planning resources for capital maintenance and net investment are raised, not by voluntary action on the part of individuals, but by State fiat. A certain part of total money income is expended by the public on the products of the State industries, and is used by the State to cover the costs of production (including wear and tear allowances and depreciation); while a certain other part is collected from the public and used by the State to set men to work in making additions to the stock of capital. Alternatively, no money levies are made directly on the public, the whole of their money income being left free for spending; but the prices of the goods sold to them are marked up in such a way that the State has available for investment whatever sum it requires in excess of the costs of production of the goods sold to the public. As a matter of fact,

---

[1] As is well known, a large proportion, not merely of the gross, but also of the net investment undertaken in this country is made by directors of companies out of undistributed profits, that have never been handed out to the public. These directors, however, though in the short run quasi-sovereigns, are in the long run agents of their shareholders.

there seems little point in the State paying out income and afterwards taking part of it back in taxes or loans. Doctoring of prices is the simpler method. Under it the planning authority is free either to add an equal percentage to all prices or to add specially low percentages for commodities whose consumption it is anxious to encourage. It may, perhaps, be objected that doctoring prices entails making equi-proportionate levies from all categories of income receivers, whereas the planning authority may not desire to do this. In that case, however, all it has to do is to make an adjustment in the amounts of income assigned to the members of selected categories. The choice of technique by which resources are set aside for capital maintenance and net investment is, however, a secondary matter. The crucial point is that, under socialist central planning, in determining the total amount to be set aside, the (voluntary) forces of demand and supply, operating through the rate of interest, are not, as they are under capitalism, the governing factor. This total amount is determined by fiat; the accounting rate of interest, which we have supposed the planning authority for its own convenience to have set up, is deliberately adjusted to this total amount, and serves only, in the manner described on p. 130 as a gauge for regulating its allocation, without surplus or deficit, among various kinds of investment. The fact that the authority chooses to establish such a rate gives no reason for supposing that the amount of investment which it will decide to make is the same as the amount which —with the type of banking policy here assumed or, indeed, with any other type—would have been made under capitalism.

Now, if it were true that the free play of self-interest under capitalism tends to bring about every year the optimum amount of capital maintenance and net investment, this would be a serious disadvantage in socialist central planning. But there is no reason for believing that that is true. The attitude towards investment of private individuals, and equally of their agents, is affected by the fact that many persons prefer present satisfactions to future satisfactions of equal intensity, even when the occurrence of the latter is certain. That preference is non-rational. Of two *equal* satisfactions the nearer is *desired* more keenly beforehand simply because it is nearer. But, of course, being equal, the two satisfactions, viewed *sub specie eternitatis*, are equally *desirable*. An arrangement which depends on a non-rational preference for the present over the future inevitably reduces investment below what, in the interest of economic welfare as a whole, it "ought" to be. It may be, no doubt, that a central planning authority would make *less* provision for investment than would be made through the private action of individuals in a similarly placed capitalist society. But the Russian experiment suggests that it is *likely* to make *more* provision. There is certainly no ground for asserting *a priori* that in this field socialist central planning will produce situations less favourable to general well-being than capitalism would do.

CHAPTER IX

CONCLUSION

THE considerations set out in the foregoing chapters are inadequate to determine our practical choice between capitalism and socialist central planning. For this there is one obvious and dominant reason. Alike under the head of capitalism and under that of socialism, a great number of detailed schemes differing in important respects are included. We are, in effect, trying to compare *some* unspecified member of one family with *some* member, also unspecified, of a different family. Unless we believe that the worst member of the one family is better than the best of the other, this is an impossible task. If, to make things easier, we take, as our representative of capitalism, the actual economic arrangements ruling in this country now and leave socialism a vague concept, we are tilting the balance against capitalism. For we are setting a nude figure, with all its blemishes patent to the eye, against a figure that is veiled. If, realising this, we replace the veiled figure by socialist central planning, as it is manifest in

Russia to-day, we are tilting the balance in the opposite sense. For Russia has always been a country enormously poorer than our own; one to a vastly greater extent engaged in agriculture; one in which in pre-socialist days the Civil Service was notoriously corrupt and popular education scandalously neglected. Moreover, the new system came into being as an immediate sequel of a disastrous foreign war; it was cradled in civil strife, and developed by means and in the midst of a widespread and tyrannous persecution. Socialist central planning introduced into England now by peaceful parliamentary process—if it could be so introduced—would, there is every reason to believe, make an enormously better showing than its Russian exemplar; just as capitalism did in the days of the Tzars. It is thus hopeless to expect, even though economic considerations alone were relevant, any sort of "demonstration" that socialist central planning either "ought" or "ought not" to be introduced into this country; and, of course, in fact many imponderables, with which economics has no concern, also bear upon the issue.

The fact, however, that we are without the data and the instruments of thought necessary for assured judgment, does not entitle us to sit back with folded hands. For to sit so is itself to take a decision; to make the great refusal, to declare ourselves in advance opponents of any change. In human affairs it is rarely possible to demonstrate absolutely—even though our criteria of "good" be agreed—that one course of action is "better" than another. The data are always imperfect. Nevertheless, having equipped ourselves with the relevant knowledge and technique, we must use these imperfect data as best we may, and take the plunge, and *judge*. There is no other way.

In this field an economist has no special qualification. Indeed, as a more or less cloistered person, he is worse qualified than many others, who, maybe, have less knowledge of the relevant facts. A wide experience of men and of affairs and a strong "feel" for what, with the human instruments available, will or will not work, are needed here. These the present writer, like most academic persons, does not possess; and, unlike some academic persons, he is aware that he does not possess them. None the less, to conclude a book like this without some sort of confession of faith on the issues with which it deals would be open to misconception. Something, however crude and tentative, must be adventured.

If, then, it were in the writer's power to direct his country's destiny, he would accept, for the time being, the general structure of capitalism; but he would modify it gradually. He would use the weapon of graduated death duties and graduated income tax, not merely as instruments of revenue, but with the deliberate purpose of diminishing the glaring inequalities of fortune and opportunity which deface our present civilisation. He would take a leaf from the book of Soviet Russia and remember that the most important investment of all is investment in the health, intelligence and character of the people. To advocate "economy" in this field would, under his government, be a criminal offence. All industries affected with a public interest, or capable of wielding monopoly power, he would subject at least to public supervision and control. Some of them, certainly the manufacture of armaments, probably the coal industry, possibly the railways, he would nationalise, not, of course, on the pattern of the Post Office, but through public boards or commissions. The Bank of England he would make in name—what it is already in effect—a public institution; with instructions to use its power to mitigate, so far as may be, violent fluctuations in industry and employment. If all went well, further steps towards nationalisation of important industries would be taken by degrees. In controlling and developing these nationalised industries, the central government would inevitably need to "plan" an appropriate allocation for a large part of the country's annual investment in new capital. When these things had been accomplished, the writer would consider his period of office at an end, and would surrender the reins of government. In his political testament he would recommend his successor also to follow the path of gradualness—to mould and transform, not violently to uproot; but he would add, in large capitals, a final sentence, that gradualness implies action, and is not a polite name for standing still.

THE END